P9-DMX-566

Williams, Cratis D.
I become a teacher

DATE DUE

~~AUG 31 98~~			
MAR 13 .			

I Become a Teacher

I Become a Teacher

A Memoir of One-Room School Life in Eastern Kentucky

by

Cratis D. Williams

Edited and with an Introduction by
James M. Gifford

The Jesse Stuart Foundation
Ashland, Kentucky
1995

Dedicated to
The School Teachers of Appalachia

Jesse Stuart Foundation
I BECOME A TEACHER
A Memoir of One-Room School Life in Eastern Kentucky
Copyright © 1995 by the Jesse Stuart Foundation

Book Design by FLEXISOFT

Library of Congress Cataloging-in-Publication Data

Williams, Cratis D.
    I become a teacher : a memoir of one-room school life in eastern Kentucky / by Cratis D. Williams ; edited and with an introduction by James M. Gifford.
        p.   cm.
    ISBN 0-945084-50-1
    1. Williams, Cratis D.   2. Educators--Kentucky--Biography.
3. Education, Rural--Kentucky--History.   I. Gifford, James M.
II. Title.
LA2317.W513A3   1995
371.1' 0092--dc20
[B]   95-7412
                                                                    CIP

Published by:
The Jesse Stuart Foundation
P.O. Box 391
Ashland, KY 41114

Acknowledgments

Colleagues and friends, too many to list individually, have provided much encouragement and assistance. To each of them I extend my heartfelt appreciation. Mistakes and shortcomings should be charged directly to my account, but dividends of praise go to all who invested good-spirited energy in this project. I offer special thanks to Jerry A. Herndon, Loyal Jones, Jim Wayne Miller, and Jerry Crouch for reading and commenting on my Introduction.

I would also like to acknowledge the gracious assistance of Cratis Williams' widow Elizabeth, son David, sister Mabel Barber, and nephew George C. Barber for providing many of the photographs used to illustrate this book. The Office of Institutional Relations at Morehead State University also shared excellent photographs.

My office staff—Chuck D. Charles, Trish Hall, and Bridget C. Tolliver—helped at every stage of production. Jim Marsh designed the dust jacket, and David and William Richmond of Flexisoft produced the camera-ready pages.

Finally, I am enormously grateful to my late friend, Cratis D. Williams, for entrusting me with the responsibility of publishing this memoir. I wish he were here to see the book in print. I think he would be greatly pleased to note that it is dedicated to the school teachers of Appalachia.

Commonwealth of Kentucky

Department of Public Instruction

Division of Certification

FRANKFORT

S 1928 № 1342

This Certifies that _Cratis D Williams_

has satisfied the legal requirements for the issuance of this Provisional Elementary Teacher's Certificate.

Basis of Issuance:—This certificate is issued on the basis of evidence showing that the holder has satisfied provisions of the General Certification Law, enacted 1926 session, Kentucky General Assembly, as evidenced by certified statement showing graduation from an accredited high school and in addition thereto certified transcript of college credits showing that the holder has credit for _36_ _(4 sem hrs. Cd.)_ semester hours from _Cumberland College_, a standard college at _Williamsburg_, _Ky_.

Validity:—This certificate is valid for teaching in the elementary schools of Kentucky for a period ending June 30, 19_31_.

Issued _June 18_, 19_29_

Approved:

Warren Peyton
Director of Certification

W A Bell
Superintendent Public Instruction

Introduction

This book is a memoir of one-room school life in 1929. Although it is set in Eastern Kentucky, it is not so much about a place as it is about a time—a time when one-room schools dotted the hills and hollows throughout the Southern mountains. While it details the first teaching experience of Cratis D. Williams, it is also a tribute to the tens of thousands of teachers like Williams who helped to resurrect the Appalachian South between 1875 and 1940. Jesse Stuart called these forgotten heroes and heroines "immortal teachers." They were natural leaders who did not allow poverty to impede their love of learning, and they passed that love on to their students when they became teachers.

Much of what has been written on one-room school life has been from the perspective of former students. These remembrances are usually humorous and often romanticized stories of "the good ol' days." In *I Become a Teacher*, Cratis Williams broadens that perspective by telling the story of one-room school life from the teacher's viewpoint.

In his day, Cratis D. Williams (1911-1985) was America's foremost scholar on the Appalachian experience. This book is the beautifully told story of his first teaching assignment at eighteen, in a one-room school on Caines Creek in Lawrence County, Kentucky. What such schools lacked in "modern conveniences," they overcame with students who were willing to endure hardships in order to learn and improve themselves, and with teachers like Cratis Williams who were dedicated champions of progress and learning.

The one-room school was once one of the greatest forces for change in Kentucky. This was particularly true in poverty-ridden Eastern Kentucky, where the tiny schools that dotted the hills and valleys were, collectively, a means of salvation for the people of an area left outside the mainstream of American life by the currents of economic progress. In the nineteenth century, these schools were located within walking distance of a few families who could pay the teacher. By the early twentieth century, when Cratis Williams took the Caines Creek School, little had changed except that the teacher was paid by the county. During the 1918-19 school year, Kentucky had 7,067 one-room schools in operation.

One-room school teachers received little recognition and few tangible rewards. Some became certified teachers by taking a qualifying examination that was developed annually by the state Department of Education and administered by the county superintendent. The one-room schoolteacher handled eight grades in the same room, and was also nurse, counselor, janitor, playground director, and "lunchroom supervisor." In spite of the hard work and long hours, the pay was very low. Some became teachers because economic and social conditions blocked other professional opportunities.

To maintain appropriate school conduct, some teachers had a lengthy catalog of rules, which specified a punishment for each infraction. Gradually, this approach to discipline improved as teachers became better trained. Many teachers did not control their classes by punitive measures. Instead, they induced their students to like them and to want to behave well to please them. Nevertheless, a teacher had to maintain credibility as a disciplinarian. If students knew they would be punished they rarely misbehaved, and if parents knew their children were fairly punished for misbehavior, they were almost always supportive of the teacher.

The routine of school life was occasionally interrupted by special social activities. Daytime events were student celebrations of holidays or scholastic competitions. Evening activities such as pie suppers were community socials that also provided operating funds for the school.

Transportation to and from school, by today's standards, ranked somewhere between inconvenient and impossible. Students and teachers usually walked. It was not uncommon for children to face a three-mile walk each way. Some teachers rode a horse or pony. Others came in a horse-drawn buggy. By the 1930s some were driving cars to school. The automobile, however, did not greatly facilitate travel in the Kentucky mountains because of the poor roads and the isolation of the schools. There were no "snow days" in the one-room schools; the teacher and the students dressed warmly and walked through the snow. For the most part, transportation difficulties were accepted as part of the rugged way of life in early twentieth-century Kentucky's rural areas. The hike to school often provided a time for unsupervised recreation for young people. The adventures they experienced became an exciting part of the history and folklore of one-room school life.

The school building was of wooden-frame construction. It typically had a front door that faced the road or path, three windows on each side of the building, and a painted blackboard across the back. Two long recitation benches faced the teacher's desk and blackboard. Rows of desks or benches, a potbellied stove, and a water bucket completed the list of basic equipment. Teachers were often quite ingenious in equipping their school buildings. For example, a teacher from Letcher County who had no timepiece in her classroom cut notches in the door frame on the east side of the building. When the sun hit the first notch, it was time to begin school. The second mark signaled recess, and the third indicated lunch time; notches on a west window marked the afternoon hours. Another cut up a calendar to help first graders learn to put the numbers in order. In many instances, the teachers spent much of their meager earnings on their school and students. "By the time I got through dressing those children and buying my materials, I never had anything left," said one former teacher. "I just might as well have been staying at home. All I was getting was experience."

Successful one-room teachers usually made good use of the skills and interests of older students. The older boys and girls often helped younger students with their lessons. Advanced students also conducted drills for lower-grade classes and supervised play activities. Many former one-room school students remember these responsibilities as good learning experiences.

Cratis Williams' teaching philosophy was unique. He assumed "that all 33 of the children [in his first school] were capable, eager, and industrious." Proceeding on that assumption, he laid down no rules, as one-room school teachers before him had always done. Rather, he referred to "the desire of everyone to be thoughtful and considerate of others and to have others return thoughtfulness and consideration."

With this as a guide, he assured his students, "we would most certainly get along well and enjoy school." Cratis was so successful in establishing his basic guidelines for conduct that the "traditional terminal punishment" for misbehavior in one-room schools, whipping a child with a switch, was unnecessary throughout the entire school year.

Cratis' keen sensitivity to other people's feelings and his compassion and appreciation for others became personal trademarks. At Caines Creek school, he had "three little towheaded girls" who could not buy toothbrushes for their oral hygiene class, and so Cratis asked their parents for permission to buy the brushes as presents.

"The father and mother looked at each other for a moment. Tears came to the mother's eyes as she nodded her head slightly." The father said that he would like "for his girls to be able to do what the other children did," and he told Cratis that the children quoted him as the "pure Gospel."

The father offered to repay him, but Cratis told him that he had not come to urge him to go into debt for the brushes, that he liked his little girls and "they were doing so well in school that he wanted to give them the brushes . . . but did not want to run the risk of hurting [the parents'] feelings," and so he sought and received their approval. On his way back home, Cratis stopped at the country store and post office and bought three toothbrushes—a green one, a blue one and a red one—so that everyone could participate in the toothbrush drill.

Throughout his career, Cratis extended this kind of loving help. I first met him in the summer of 1977 at a Berea College workshop in Appalachian history and literature. I had heard of him long before I met him, but, unlike many living legends, he measured up to his reputation. He enthralled audiences with his knowledge, and he captivated individuals with his charm. Not surprisingly, I was eager to involve him when I went to Morehead State University in 1978 to develop an Appalachian Studies Program.

The following fall (November 28-30, 1979) Cratis served as a consultant at MSU's Appalachian Development Center. As always, he kept a hectic schedule gracefully. He met with the Appalachian Studies Advisory Committee, delivered a public lecture one evening, addressed several classes, and met informally with interested students and faculty. Afterwards, he submitted a detailed set of guidelines that provided intellectual, curricular, and developmental cornerstones for our emerging program.

His greatest effect, however, was on the individuals he encountered. One faculty member wrote to him: "Words have not the power to convey either my joy from or the positive effect of your three-day visit to our campus . . . I am delighted to have met a person with your knowledge of our cultural heritage and zest for sharing it with others. I eagerly await your next visit to Morehead." Another wrote that his lecture to her literature class "provided one of the finest academic experiences that our students could ever have."

In June of 1980 and 1981 and again in 1984, Williams served as Scholar in Residence for MSU's annual Appalachian Celebration. He delivered the first address in MSU's "Our Mountain Heritage" lecture series on September 17, 1981. I was impressed with his wide-ranging knowledge and with his enormous personal charisma. Again, his contributions were great and far-reaching and the positive effects of his visits were felt throughout the area long after he returned to his home in Boone, North Carolina, where he remained actively "retired" as a special assistant to the chancellor of Appalachian State University.

Between 1977 and 1981, Cratis and I became good friends and he took a genuine interest in my personal life as well as in my professional accomplishments. Having grown up without a father or grandfather in my home, I truly appreciated his kind and nurturing support, and I was always pleased to introduce him to my friends and to include him in dinner plans, where he was always the "star attraction" because of his likable ways and story-telling genius.

Cratis and I often taught together. He was patient with my lectures, normally allowing that "for the most part," he agreed with what I had said. I, on the other hand, was amazed at both his knowledge and his presentation skills, and I learned a great deal from this man who was affectionately dubbed "Mr. Appalachia" by the press. Some basic information on Williams' life will help the reader understand this great man in historical context. I would not presume to tell Cratis Williams' story, since he can tell it so much

The Story Teller.   MSU Photo.

The Teacher.   MSU Photo.

better than I can. Consequently, this work concludes with an autobiographical section.

Our conversations inevitably turned to scholarship, for that was our greatest common interest. In 1983, Cratis entrusted me with a memoir, which I edited for publication by Morehead State University's Appalachian Development Center. *William H. Vaughan: A Better Man Than I Ever Wanted to Be* extolled the virtues of his high school principal, who would in 1940 become the President of Morehead State University. Cratis detailed much of his own life in this book, too. Later, he also charged me with the responsibility of publishing this memoir, *I Become a Teacher*.

Cratis' contributions to Morehead State University exemplify the type of assistance he gave throughout Eastern Kentucky. He worked closely with Ron Daley and Mike Mullins in their oral history project at Alice Lloyd College and with the late Leonard Roberts, a folklorist and publisher, at Pikeville College. He regularly taught in Berea College's highly regarded summer workshops, working with a distinguished faculty that included Loyal Jones, Richard Drake, Wilma Dykeman, Jim Wayne Miller, and many other leaders of the Appalachian Studies movement. He served on the Board of Directors of the Hindman Settlement School and as chairman of the Alumni Board of Cumberland College. His contributions to Eastern Kentucky institutions illustrate the service he provided throughout Southern Appalachia.

Although he received many honors and awards (including honorary doctorates from Morehead State University, Berea College, and Marshall University), Cratis Williams' most significant awards were not inscribed on plaques or printed handsomely on diplomas or books. They were written with love and admiration on the hearts of hundreds of people like me who are forever grateful for his friendship, advice, and good company.

Williams died on May 12, 1985, following a three-year battle

Cratis Williams lecturing at Morehead State University.   MSU Photo.

with cancer. His body was cremated and his ashes were spread to the winds at his family cemetery near Blaine in Lawrence County, Kentucky. I spoke at his burial service, and I have thought of him often during the last decade. Like Tennyson's Ulysses, Cratis Williams became a part of all that he met. The part of us that is Cratis is now more than a gift; it is a responsibility.

The following memoir offers eloquent testimony to Cratis Williams' teaching excellence and to his great love for the people of Southern Appalachia. It is a book that may inspire some people to become teachers, and it may encourage others to remain in the profession. As Americans address current school problems, we must realize that we cannot solve today's educational dilemma simply by pumping more money into the system. Real success will come when we somehow find a way to develop more teachers and more administrators like Cratis Williams.

James M. Gifford
February 20, 1995

Principal of Blaine High School.
Courtesty of the Williams Family Collection.

I Become a Teacher

During my first year in college at Cumberland I took courses needed to qualify at the end of the year for a certificate to teach in elementary schools. My father asked Arb Gambill, the local trustee of the Boggs School on Caines Creek, whether he would recommend me to teach the school for 1929-1930. Arb, recognizing that I was only eighteen years old and small for my age, agreed to recommend me. Ora Boggs, who had taught the school for three years, did not want to continue. My father wrote to tell me that I had a school for next year.

It would be possible for me to teach the school, which would begin the last Monday in July and end the first week in February, and return to college for the second semester and the first summer term. If I should get along all right and like teaching, I could continue as a one-room school teacher and, by living at home, sharing the evening and morning chores, and helping out on Saturdays, not have to pay for board and room. This arrangement would enable me to save my salary money to pay my college expenses for the second semester and summer term each year.

Knowing that I had a job for the following year stimulated my interest in the education courses that I had been permitted to include as an extra load at Cumberland College to add up a total of 36 semester hours for the year. Professor A. R. Evans' course in classroom management, geared specifically to the needs of one-room teachers in the mountains, became one of my most exciting courses. Even Mr. Creech's course in arithmetic and how to teach it generated so much enthusiasm that I overcame my feeling of inadequacy in mathematics and made an A in the course.

Not having financial resources for continuing in summer school for the first term at Cumberland, I came home after the academic year ended. It had been necessary that I write my father for enough money to pay for shipping my things home and my railroad ticket to Webbville. The year had been difficult for me financially. My wardrobe was shabby and there had been little money for enjoying such extras as outings to Cumberland Falls or Corbin or Jellico.

When I arrived at Webbville, I arranged for the mail carrier to bring my battered old suitcase, the same one my father had given me when he had taken me out to high school five years earlier, on the mail wagon. I walked the eleven miles from Webbville to our home.

The family was preparing to sit down to dinner when I reached home. Mr. Webb, the horseback drummer who spent one night a month at our home, was there. The dinner, better than what we usually had, was much better than any I had eaten for a long time, and I was uncommonly hungry. I had eaten only an egg sandwich for breakfast.

After dinner, I changed clothes, found my hoe, and went into the cornfield with the family, for we were "digging the corn out of the first weeds." The corn that year had been planted in a 30-acre steep hillside field that had been in pasture for several years but, as my father said, needed to be "plowed and corned a year or two and then regrassed." The sun was hot, the rows were long, my hands were tender, and my muscles were soft. The afternoon seemed interminably long to me. As I lagged behind with the top row, my father would comment, mostly, I thought, for my grandfather, who had come to help with the corn until his was ready to hoe. Not wanting to seem inadequate, I drove myself onward, even though my legs were trembling and the blisters in my hands were bursting, causing my hands to stick to the hoe handle. We had one rest period of about fifteen minutes in the middle of the afternoon.

That evening I resumed the share of chores that I had always done while I was at home. The supper, also better than we normally had because Mr. Webb was spending the night with us, was eaten by lamplight. I was so tired that I did not have much interest in it.

That night held little rest for me. My sunburned neck and arms, galled hands, tired back, and sore leg muscles made it painful for me to move, but the most disturbing aspect of it all was the continuing feeling that I was still hoeing corn. Just as I was about to go to sleep my arms would flounce as if I were sinking a hoe into the earth, and I would wake up.

Next morning I was sore and stiff and my eyes were almost swollen together, but I "hit the floor a-runnin'" at my father's voice and did the chores that I had always done at home.

June and July were hard months for me. After the "first weeds" came haying, that year requiring longer than usual, for all 35 acres of bottom land was in meadow. "Second weeds" did not take as long as the first hoeing, since we did not have to thin or replant, but then came cutting stove wood for the following year. We laid the corn crop by only a few days before I was to report to Louisa for the teachers institute. But I had become tough and wiry and was as suntanned as a country boy ever becomes.

I had no money. Nothing was said about whether I should have any. As the end of July drew near, I began to think about what I might wear to Louisa and whether it might me possible for me to go a day early so I could visit with some of those who had graduated from high school in my class. I was too proud to mention money to my father, who had borne down hard on me all summer as if he were harboring some resentment against me.

Checking my wardrobe, I found that all of my pants either had holes in the seat or were perilously threadbare. I had a pair of blue serge pants, threadbare in the seat, that one of the boys at college had given me because he did not have the thirty cents he owed me for carrying his mail up from the post office. I had tried the pants on once. They fit me except that the legs were too long. My mother agreed to adjust the legs and to use the cut off pieces to quilt inside the seat. She did such a neat job that the pants looked new after I had pressed them. The darning in the seat was not readily visible. She also loaned me three dollars of her butter-and-egg money.

I decided that I did not have enough money to plan for an extra day at Louisa. On the morning of the institute I rose early, bathed in the washtub in the smokehouse shed, put on a white shirt for which my mother had turned the collar, my blue serge pants, and my dress shoes, now with the soles rolling up at the sides and the heels worn down, and walked to Blaine, five miles away, to ride to town in Lon McKinnon's "bus," a touring car into which he could crowd six passengers for a dollar each if some were willing to sit on the laps of others. The bus left Blaine at 8:30.

We arrived in Louisa in time for me to stroll up and down the street in front of the courthouse twice before the institute began in the courtroom. I had not been back to Louisa since the preceding September, but no changes in the appearance of the town had occurred. I saw none of my old classmates on the streets or in the drug stores, but I exchanged greetings with some of the older men I had known, mostly those who liked to come and sit on the ice cream cans and cartons that the merchants set on the sidewalks to be picked up by delivery boys and draymen.

Knowing that I had only two dollars of my mother's egg money in my pocket, that I had on a shirt with a turned collar, and that the pants I was wearing had been accepted in lieu of a 30-cent debt and were darned in the seat, I was relieved that I had not met any of my classmates. I felt shabbily dressed and was convinced that I looked that way, too, but I felt good about my preparation for teaching, my ability to handle a school, and my future. After I had received a check or two, I could dress myself up and not feel shy in the presence of any of my classmates or the people in town who had known me while I was a high school student here.

Promptly at ten o'clock Dock Jordan, the superintendent of schools, appeared on the balcony above the courthouse door and announced that the teachers meeting was about to begin in the courtroom. Dock looked good to me. I had been seeing him at least once a year since he first visited the one-room school I attended when I was eight years old. He had changed very little in those ten years. His steel-rimmed glasses perched on his high nose, his shirt sleeves held in place by black elastic armbands, his substantial suspenders holding up durable dark pants, and his white collar with no tie all looked the same as always.

I was one of many who went trooping through the hall, up the resounding steps of the wide stairway, and into the courtroom, where most of the teachers of the county's 100 one-room schools had already assembled. Old-timers were taking seats by tables at which lawyers sat during court. Many of them, like Grammar Ike Cunningham, Joe Swetnam, Add Skeens, Charley Sparks, Elliott Sparks, Hence Van Horn, I knew. Near them in the jury box and elsewhere sat less venerable teachers, middle aged, they seemed to me, but proud to possess a first-class certificate issued on the basis of performance on the county teachers examination. Among them were Fred Steele, Otis Bailey, Little Jesse Cordle, and Little Georgie Bishop. These were seasoned teachers, many of whom had never gone to high school but had kept their credentials in order by attending teacher institutes or normal schools for a few weeks in late winter, or by studying *Lusby's County Examiner* as they found time, to prepare themselves for the examinations. They appeared aggressive and confident.

Scattered about on the benches in the courtroom were middle-aged women, who deferred to such giants as Grammar Ike, Joe Swetnam, Add Skeens, and Hence Van Horn and would not presume to seat themselves among them at an institute. Neophytes and those who had taught only a year or two sat among the women or generally tried to make themselves as inconspicuous as possible by retreating toward the back of the room, where they sat scattered about in loneliness with much seat room between them and their neighbors. These younger teachers held certificates issued by the state department on the basis of high school credits, some earned by taking correspondence courses, normal school credits, or college semester hours. They felt inferior to the gladiators who had triumphed in the arena of examinations, the heroes who deplored the lowering of standards and the deterioration of quality that result from issuing timid girls certificates because they had ground out some high school units or college credits.

I took a seat at the end of a bench and near the center aisle four or five rows from the front. No one sat near me, either on the bench in front of me or behind me. Among the crowd I saw three or four young teachers whom I had known in high school, all looking ill at ease and uncommunicative.

Two young women, possibly sisters, whom I did not know, sat together in arm chairs near a window. They had had the audacity to take positions within the railed enclosure where the court sat, but they were far removed from the cluster of tried-in-the-traces old wheelhorses who lounged about in the chairs occupied by attorneys when the court was in session. The young women smiled at each other frequently and wrote notes to each other on a pad that the light-haired one held on her knees.

Sitting quite apart from others and on the end next to the wall of the bench in the first row was someone who looked familiar to me, a young fellow with a shock of brown hair that rose in a wave to one side of his large head. He appeared to be attempting to attract the attention of the two young women sitting together near the window but they were carefully ignoring him. He had a voice that was oddly at variance with his slight frame and which he had difficulty lowering to a whisper. After trying to communicate with the young women, he would turn around and address himself to others closest to him, his voice rattling with a deliberate and affected precision but with only an occasional word reaching me clearly. His face was animated and his mouth curled in a smile shaped like the moon in its last phase when he paused to assess the response to what he was saying. The young women at the window stole swift glances at him when he turned his head away from them but assumed a dignified poise in profile as he turned his head in their direction. Just before Dock Jordan appeared in the courtroom with two well-dressed young men flanking him, the young fellow threw his hand up at me and called my name. I recognized him as Paul Alexander, recently returned from Berea Academy, who would be teaching the Upper Caines Creek School. He lived on Lick Fork across the hill from my home. We had played together when we were little boys.

Dock Jordan took his position behind the judge's desk and called the meeting to order. Someone offered an invocation and one of the young men who had come in with the superintendent led us in the singing of "America, the Beautiful," which we did most awkwardly and uncertainly despite the efforts of the old-timers to lift the roof with their volume, but Dock, feeling patriotic and not disposed to comment on the quality of our performance, asked the young man whether he would lead us also in the singing of "The Battle Hymn of the Republic." We sang that with more confidence, especially the chorus, but I was amused to note that

Otis Bailey, his face shedding the passion of an evangelist who has been descended upon by the Holy Spirit, sounded deliberately the "w" in "sword." By crackies, a letter appearing in the spelling of a word deserves to be pronounced, he demonstrated emphatically.

Dock then welcomed us, congratulated the beginners on their achievements, assured them of their success, and emphasized the importance of stressing spelling, language, and arithmetic in teaching elementary school children. He had arranged to have three experienced and successful teachers talk to us for about five minutes each about the techniques they used in teaching these subjects. He would be pleased to entertain questions for up to five minutes after each presentation.

The first presenter was Joe Swetnam, who told how he taught spelling. His primary pupils learned to pronounce by syllables and spell each new word that appeared in the readers. He emphasized the importance of oral spelling, the value of pronouncing words clearly, the spirit of competitiveness that may be developed by having children stand in line to spell, the awarding of headmarks, the enjoyment youngsters find in spelling matches on Friday afternoons.

When he sat down, Dock asked for questions. The light-haired young woman by the window rose and asked whether there might be value in having children write words rather than spell them aloud. Mr. Swetnam rose and faced the young woman. "A child that can spell a word aloud can write it," he said sternly. "A teacher can waste a lot of time fooling with papers, and children in this county are poor. If their parents have to spend money for tablet paper for their children to waste time with, they will not send them to school."

But the young woman was not intimidated. "In practice, people spell only when they write," she responded. "At Berea we were told to teach spelling beginning with the third grade only by having pupils write words." She sat down. Mr. Swetnam was stunned. He peered about like an owl for someone who might rise to his defense.

Dock Jordan asked whether there were other questions or comments. There were none.

Grammar Ike was presented. He lifted his glasses up to the middle of his forehead, rose at his seat, and emphasized the value of parsing and diagramming as methods for teaching children to understand sentence structure. He feared for the future of education in the county because high schools and colleges were abandoning both methods. He did not comprehend what was being offered in their place but the best he could make of it was that teachers were calling on their students for little papers that did not amount to anything. "A person who can parse and diagram can write," he avowed. He had pupils in the third grade who could diagram simple and compound sentences, spreading them all over the blackboard, he said with a wide but self-caressing gesture. There was style in his delivery. His rhetoric rolled like that of a political orator. He was a master of elocutionary tricks. No one offered to challenge him or speak for any value that might exist in concentrating on actual writing as a technique for teaching sentence structure. He smiled in his self-assurance and the old heads nodded sagely.

Add Skeens spoke on his successful techniques in teaching arithmetic. He required his primary pupils to master number combinations until they could do the page in the book perfectly within three minutes before they were permitted to move on. It was absolutely necessary, he declared, that every student master the multiplication tables before moving on. These skills in hand, children would have little trouble with what came later in the arithmetic curriculum. Less skilled in oratory than Swetnam and Cunningham, he was nonetheless sure of himself and his methods. Young teachers seemed more threatened by him than they had by either of the other speakers, but no one found enough courage to either challenge or question.

The light-haired woman by the window smiled enigmatically

and wrote a note for her sister to read after each had spoken. No doubt she felt that it was not polite for her to challenge more than one of the elders.

Dock Jordan then introduced Mr. Jaggers, the rugged-faced young man who had come into the courtroom with him. Mr. Jaggers, who represented the State Department of Public Instruction in Frankfort, undertook to explain a new system of grading that the Department was asking teachers to adopt, a system in which students were assigned letter grades of A, B, C, D, and F rather than percentages. This system, Mr. Jaggers declared, is based on the assumption that an unselected group of students will have in it a few who will perform outstandingly, a few who will perform better than most but fall short of excellence, a large number, perhaps up to half, who will do work of average quality, a number who will barely meet minimum standards, and a few who will not perform even minimally. Better high schools and many of the colleges in the state were using the new system and finding it much more satisfactory than the percentage system. In the newer system, about four of every ten pupils selected at random would receive a grade of C, about two a B, about two a D, and one each an A and an F. He referred to a "normal curve" in grading and declared that it is similar to the ranges in height or weight of children of a given age.

Young teachers present, particularly those who had gone to high school or taken college courses, lit up at Mr. Jaggers' recommendation. Older teachers were disturbed. They challenged the system because it seemed not to hold the promise of an A for every student who worked for perfect mastery of a subject. Another thought it required that some students would have to fail and others make only D. Parents would not understand it. It did not assure rewards for children who studied hard.

Mr. Jaggers countered by saying that things naturally fall into a distribution like the normal curve. This grading system is more humane than the percentage system in that it does not require a teacher, for example, to fail a child with an average of 59½ percent for arithmetic when 60 percent is considered passing.

Questioned about the concept of normal distribution, Mr. Jaggers expressed the opinion that ten of the beginning teachers that year would range in height from about 5 feet 2 inches to about 6 feet 2 inches but that about five of the ten would tend to be within an inch or two of 5 feet 8 inches. To illustrate his point, he called for a show of hands of those who were beginning teachers that year. He then picked out several to come to the front of the room and lined them up according to height. Having some difficulty with the short end of the line, he turned toward the audience and asked, "Where is that little fellow I saw running around here before we came together?"

Paul Alexander, already in the line and smiling like a quarter moon but second or third from the bottom of the short end, responded oratorically, "That was Cratis Williams. Back there he sits."

Mr. Jaggers asked me to stand at the end of the line. Having observed that the young women by the window were taking a keen interest in proceedings, I half feared that they might notice that the seat of my pants had been quilted and my shoe heels were all but worn away when I took my position at the end of the line and with my back turned toward them. There was unrestrained laughter when I took my position. Then Mr. Jaggers maneuvered a short woman, not much more than 5 feet tall into position at the end of the line.

"If we were to consider height of 6 feet 2 inches excellent and height below 5 feet," he paused. "How tall are you, young man?"

"Five feet four," I responded. (There was more laughter.)

"Four as poor, unacceptable," he continued, "then this man," he pointed to the tall man at the head of the line, "would be evaluated A. This young woman," he said as he darted to the opposite end of the line and placed his hand on her head, "would be evaluated F."

There was more laughter from the audiences as the young woman made a wry face.

"These five persons," he said pointing to each, "would be C's, these two," pointing at six-footers below the tall man at the head of the line, "would be B's, and this little fellow," as he darted back to me, "would be D." Everybody laughed.

We sat down, but instead of returning to my former seat I dropped onto a bench in the front row.

Dock Jordan then introduced Mr. Grier who had led the singing. He represented Silver, Burdett and Company and had come to present to us a series of graded music books that included songs and singing games that had been taken from the collection of Jean Thomas, the Traipsin' Woman, who would become nationally known a few years later for her American Folksong Festival held the first Sunday in June at her Traipsin' Woman Cabin in Boyd County a few miles north of Louisa. A slender and handsome young fellow, he was dressed in a light summer suit. He held up the song books, identified them as to grade levels, and read from the tables of contents a few of the titles. Then he produced a pitch pipe and attempted to interest the group in singing a few of the songs. Some of the young women responded to his entreaties, but the elders sat in rigid silence and with fixed stares.

Not overwhelmed by the response to his efforts to lead us in song, he then turned to some of the singing games. Once, for a game recommended for adolescents, he broke into a lively jig as he circled about to the tune of his own voice. The young women were fascinated, but the men suffered him in silence, it seemed to me. Calling attention to his display of books, he invited interested persons to come by and look at them. He would take orders for them. The books were only 35 cents each, as I recall. I looked at them but did not feel that I could risk spending 35 cents of my mother's butter-and-egg money for one of the books.

Dock Jordan then concluded the meeting. He reminded us of the necessity for submitting at the end of each month an attendance report, forms for which would be found in the record book to be issued after lunch. He tried to get around to visiting each of the schools at least once during the seven-month term, he said, but he would not be able to let us know ahead of time when he might appear. Usually, he could visit up to four schools a day, but if the weather should be bad and roads muddy, he might sometimes not be able to visit more than two or three a day. Some years he was not able to get around to every school because of increased work in his office. He had no assistant and only one secretary. Plans were underway to establish three rural high schools that year, one at Blaine, one at Webbville, and one at Clifford. We were asked to urge young people in our communities who had finished grade school or were continuing to come to the grade schools to repeat upper-grade work because they had been unable to go away to high school to take advantage of opportunities being made available to them.

We should come back at one o'clock and check out our supplies. That year we would receive a record book, one box of chalk, two erasers, a broom, a ten-quart galvanized water bucket, and a tin dipper. Our local trustees would arrange to have coal delivered to our schools before cold weather. There was no money for books and instructional materials. Many teachers raised money for these by holding pie mites and cake walks. If we should decide to do this, a good company to order materials from was A. Flanagan in Chicago. He gave us the street address so we could order catalogs if we were interested. We were dismissed.

Teachers scattered in many directions. Some went to dust-covered Model T Ford cars parked around the courthouse square, got lunches they had brought with them, and ate, some sitting in their cars and some on seats scattered about the square. A few of the younger ones went to sandwich shops. I went to a little restaurant off the main street and had a cheese sandwich and a Nehi. I was the only teacher there at lunch time.

At one o'clock I went by and checked out my supplies. Lon McKinnon was ready to return to Blaine when I was. He had only two or three passengers besides myself.

With the broom in one hand and the bucket, into which I had packed the chalk, erasers, dipper, and record book, in the other, I walked the five miles from Blaine to our home.

I was now a teacher. I recall the cool, dank stretches of the sandy road beside Blaine Creek and the dust on the tall weeds and the leaves on the sycamores, willows, and water birches as I strolled along. Occasionally, I would be blinded by the dust kicked up by a car, but after I turned up the Caines Creek road I saw no more cars. The afternoon was hot. Poison ivy along the fence rows and the trumpet flowers that dipped from the Virginia Creeper growing on posts were still and dark in the hot sun. I thought of my trip up the creek in the wagon a year and a half before when I held proudly on my knee the loving cup I had received at the high school commencement and how pleased I had been to find on the front page of the *Big Sandy News* a week later my picture and a writeup that Earl Kinner had prepared. I remembered the trip in the wagon less than a year before when my father brought me to Blaine to find a ride to Louisa where I left by train for Cumberland College. That had been a hard but pleasant year, for all of that. I had made good grades, earned extra credits, and felt confident that I would teach a good school. I had also felt more keenly the pinch of poverty and recognized more deeply than ever before that I was depressed much of the time. The running sore on my thigh had never healed. My left leg tired easily. But I also knew that I felt irrepressible joy, especially with other people, and that I would go on to the University of Kentucky where I would have the money I had earned as a teacher to support me without my having to try to work and go to college at the same time.

My shirt was wet with sweat and soiled from the dust and my pants were heavy on my hips and dusty to the knees when I reached home about four o'clock. I changed to a hickory shirt and overalls and went to the schoolhouse to tidy it up for the beginning of the school the following morning. I threw up the windows, tore away nests of wasps and dirt-daubers, swept the floor, dusted the desks and the cottage organ that the school had bought the previous year with money raised at a pie mite. I pumped water from the well, and I found it clean and cool. The schoolyard, sitting in the edge of the pasture, had not been fenced off from the rest of the field. The farmer pumped water from the well for his cattle. The cattle had kept the grass grazed down and the weeds away.

I fetched the coal bucket and fire shovel from one of the cloakrooms and shoveled up and carried away the fresher piles of manure left around the house by the cattle. Then I cut away the taller weeds and bushes that had grown up around and through the steps of the style over the pasture fence by which one gained access to the schoolyard. The two-holer toilets, each with a box of old papers and catalogs children had contributed the year before in place on the floor beside the door, had a stench rising from the pits. I dug sand from the bed of the branch behind them and covered the decaying excretion in each pit.

Everything in order at the school, I returned home in time to do my share of the chores. After supper I sat at the dining room table and I wrote out on theme paper a plan for the first day of school.

Thirty-three children and two parents, one the local trustee, reported. Four were beginners and eight were in the eighth grade. Among my pupils were my brother and sister, my aunt, four years younger than I, four of my first cousins, and many, only a year or two younger than myself, with whom I had been in school and played on weekends before I left to go to high school. Several of

Cratis Williams and his brothers and sisters attended the Boggs School long before Cratis taught there. Above, fifth from right in the front row is Cratis' sister Mabel. The little fellow in the hat, fourth from the left in the front row, is Cratis. The teacher, the tallest person in the back row, is Ulysses Williams, Cratis' second cousin.

Courtesy of the Williams Family Collection

them, both boys and girls, were taller and heavier than I. At eighteen I weighed only 118 pounds and was 5 feet 4 inches tall.

I had dressed myself in my quilted pants and a clean blue shirt with an open collar. The boys were dressed in overalls and hickory shirts, the girls in clean gingham and calico. All were barefoot.

One of my "innovations," which all liked, was to seat grades in sections so I could have all of those in the same grade together for convenience in supervising written exercises. I would not always call them to the recitation bench but would, instead, come to their section to conduct discussion. Always they had sat boys on one side of the room and girls on the other and gone to the recitation bench for "reciting." The idea of sitting two at a desk, boys at one and girls at another, appealed to them. But I told them that this arrangement was an experiment and that if I learned it did not work well we could return to the seating arrangement with which they were familiar and use the recitation bench as they had always done.

Another of my innovations was to march the entire student body into the schoolyard after lessons for the first three grades in the afternoon for ten minutes of breathing, bending, and stretching exercises to tone them up and help them overcome the drowsiness from which students suffer after lunch. They liked this and became competitive in acquiring skill in touching their toes with their fingers in the bending exercises.

Not all of the pupils owned books, but those who had books were placed to share them with seat mates. I did not have a complete set of books for all grades myself. It was necessary for me to borrow books from students to use in making lesson plans. Except for an ancient unabridged dictionary and two or three old hymnals at the organ, there were no books in the school building at all.

The matter of whether I would be able to handle any discipline problems in the school did not bother me. I assumed that all thirty-three of the children were capable, eager, and industrious. Proceeding on that assumption, I laid down no rules, as one-room teachers had always done when I had been a pupil, but referred to the desire of everyone to be thoughtful and considerate of others and to have others return thoughtfulness and consideration. With this as a guide, we would most certainly get along well and enjoy school. I was so successful in presenting my basic guideline for conduct that it was not necessary all year to whip a child with a switch, the traditional terminal punishment for misbehavior in one-room schools.

Four of the eight in the 8th grade had taken eighth grade before. It soon became apparent to me that they should be encouraged to consider enrolling at the high school scheduled to open at the beginning of September at Blaine. The other four, though not excellent students, were old enough to be in high school and ought to be encouraged, it seemed to me, to go. I had not completed 8th grade myself, I reminded them, and I had graduated from high school second in my class of 41. They could succeed if they were willing to try. I invited all of them to discuss the matter with their parents.

The possibility that they might go to high school was keen motivation for them. They would report on the progress being made in discussions at home about their going. They could walk, but all of them had horses or mules they could ride. Mr. Hewlette, who had a large barn in which he kept only a cow, a hog, and a few chickens, would permit them to leave their horses in stables in his barn without charging them anything. They could leave their lunches in their saddlebags, return from the high school at lunch time and water their horses and feed them corn from the saddlebags, eat their own simple lunches, and get back to school all during the one-hour lunch break. One by one they reported that I could let David Morris, the principal of the school, know that they would be there.

The day before I was to report to Mr. Morris, my aunt Elva, one of the better students, despondent and disappointed, told me secretly that Grandpa did not want her to go to high school. He had not yet said she could not, but he had talked against it every time she mentioned it. I asked whether she would approve of my talking with Grandpa about it. She was pleased that I was willing to do so.

That afternoon, after I had done my share of the chores at home, I walked down to Grandpa's to talk with him. He had not yet come in from riving boards for a new roof on a part of his barn. I went to the woodlot where he was working. When I mentioned what I had come for, he laid his maul and fro on an upended cut from the tree, and we sat down on the hillside. Since girls marry and start keeping house and raising youngens, he could not see how a high school education would help them any. It would be money lost to pay for books and clothes and meet other expenses that would be coming up all the time.

I began saying that my aunt was a good student and a bright girl. She was ready for high school and wanted to go. She was as bright as any of them. Sending her would not really cost much, probably not more than $15.00 or $20.00 for the whole year. She had a good horse to ride, and she could wait for the other students each morning and all of them could ride down to Blaine together. Lon Hewlette had agreed to let all of them put their horses in his barn without charge.

But Grandpa had sent Estill to school and it had been a waste of money. None of the others had gone. Times were hard. He was getting old. Unless a girl made a teacher of herself, the time and money for going to high school would be wasted. He sat musing to himself for a few minutes. I waited in silence. "Well, if she has her head set on it, I'll let her go," he said. "I reckon she had as well try it as Arb Gambill's and Lon Boggs's girls. If you say I ought to send her, I'll let her go."

Elva was waiting for me in the yard. When I told her that

Grandpa had agreed to let her go, she was so happy that she cried.

After I had been teaching two or three weeks, my brother came from his desk one morning and whispered to me that his seatmate was so drunk that he could not sit up. I looked at the boy, slumped in his seat, pale, and his neck so limber that his head was dangling. I observed that I believed the boy was sick and might feel better if he should lie down for a little while. He nodded his head weakly. My brother and Ora Gambill helped him leave the room and went with him to a grass-covered spot in the shade of a tree beyond the branch, where they laid him out to sleep.

Everybody was concerned. Ora and my brother reported that the boy was sick and vomiting. The girls thought he should be taken home. Ora explained that he could not walk then, but when he began to feel better he would be glad to walk home with him. Ora thought the boy would feel better, now that he had vomited the sickness off his stomach, after he had slept a while.

At the recess period I went out to see the boy. He had been sleeping, but the noise of the children at play had awakened him. He felt better, he said, and would go home by himself in a little while. At the noon hour I went back and found that he had left. I made no reference to his intoxication, nor did Ora or my brother Ralph. The next day the boy was back at school. I never mentioned the "sickness" to his parents nor they to me, and the boy and I never referred to it subsequently. It is possible that the parents never knew that their son had either slipped into his father's supply of whiskey or taken drinks with someone he had met on the way to school. I felt good about my discretion in handling a sensitive situation and was pleased that Ora and Ralph, without my advising them in any way, kept the boy's secret and that he did not feel that he should explain his behavior to me. It was as if all three of them were as eager to hold from me knowledge that I might feel compelled to act on as I was that they not tell me. The boy had not misbehaved in any way and had created no disturbance during his brief spree of "public drunkenness." It was better for him, I thought, that as little attention as possible be called to his mistake.

One noon hour while we were all playing a ring game in the schoolyard, a shining new car stopped beside the road. A well-dressed man got out of the driver's seat and a tall woman dressed in white got out on the other side. As the man crossed the style, I advanced toward him. That day I was dressed in white ducks and a white sport shirt, which might have set me apart in appearance from boys of the school, many of them larger than I but all of whom wore hickory shirts and overalls.

"Hey, sonny, where's your teacher?" the man asked, while the woman was peering around him with a smile.

"I am the teacher," I responded. The children laughed gleefully and the man was embarrassed.

He was the county health officer and the woman was the nurse. They had come to vaccinate for smallpox, inoculate for other diseases, and examine the children's tonsils. Many of the small children were frightened, but with the encouragement of older brothers and sisters and soft words from me all of them were examined and inoculated. One pale little girl fainted, but the nurse took charge of her and had her laughing in a few minutes.

The doctor explained as he was ready to leave that in many schools some of the children absolutely refused to submit to examination and that ours was one of only a few in which there had been one hundred percent cooperation.

When I was at Blaine later, Lon Hewlette reported that the doctor had told at the table in Mrs. Hewlette's boarding house about embarrassing himself by asking me where the teacher was but reported that I had one of the best schools he had yet visited.

Beard was not yet growing on most of my face, but my mustache and a few chin whiskers had sprouted and I was shaving away the fuzz about twice a week. I resolved to grow a mustache in order to give me the appearance of being older than I was. For two or three years my mustache was thin and downy looking, but I kept it trimmed and lined neatly and darkened it with mascara when I dressed up. I have worn a mustache most of the time since then and was never mistaken for one of my students again.

Anticipating that there would be no teaching materials available to me, I had saved at college the laundry cards around which shirts were returned and brought a supply of them home with me. As I found time, I cut the cards into strips which I used as blanks for flash cards. I had no broad pen points and no india ink, but I would letter carefully with a pencil and then widen the lines with a fountain pen and blue ink. As children in the first and second grades were introduced to new words in their readers, I prepared flash cards with those words on them. Older girls in the school would take the small children into the cloakroom and play cards with them. I also prepared cards with number combinations to help them master simple sums.

After the A. Flanagan catalog arrived, I studied it carefully. Flash cards of all kinds, duplicating equipment, art materials, supplementary readers, and graded story books were available at reasonable prices. For as little as twenty dollars one could get enough material to enrich doubly what was available in the textbooks. I told the students about what was available and permitted them to study the catalog.

We decided to have a pie mite to raise money for teaching materials, supplementary readers, and a few library books. Since our own schoolhouse was in the edge of a pasture field and it was difficult, with cattle in the pasture and often rubbing against the corners of the building while school was in session, to accommodate horseback riders and those who might want to come in wagons at the school, we would hold our pie mite at the church house, in which the school had been held, too, until a new building for it had been constructed only a year before. There was room at the church house for horses and wagons and a big crowd of people.

We arranged to use the church house the last Saturday night in August. I wrote to teachers of neighboring schools and asked that they announce our pie mite and cake walk and that there would be a string band to furnish music for the cake walk. I invited Dick Sturgill to bring his fiddle and two or three boys to play banjos, guitars, and mandolins with him. My father agreed to "cry off" the pies.

The eighth graders would not be returning to the school following the pie mite, but they helped to prepare for it. One of the girls agreed to bake a cake for the walk and another to bake a pie for the guessing contest. The pie for the guessing contest would be filled with something edible but that nobody would want to eat. Big sisters of courting age, unmarried aunts, eligible young men no longer in school were urged to come to the mite, which would begin at seven o'clock.

My father in a burst of generosity had invited me to let Dick Sturgill take my measurements for a new suit, one with an extra pair of pants, for $21.50. I needed a new suit, my father had said, and I had worked hard all summer. He would buy the suit for me and I could save my money for college expenses. The suit, a neatly fitting dark blue with a pencil stripe, had arrived only two or three days before the pie mite. I wore it for the first time and had never felt better dressed in my life.

The crowd began to gather by five o'clock. Old ladies from other communities came bearing pies in pans or plates on their extended hands for starry-eyed daughters and nieces, dressed in fresh gingham or voile, who walked beside them, their new shoes creaking and their shapely legs flashing the flesh color of lisle stockings.

The old ladies would deposit the pies, to which strips of paper bearing the names of the owners had been stuck, on long benches beside the pulpit. Young fellows, dressed in their best, rode their horses around the church house and selected flying limbs of beech trees to hitch them to. They gathered around the front door of the church, where they stood, skillfully rolling cigarettes. They poured tobacco from little cloth bags with yellow drawstrings with tags on them then they closed the bags by holding the string with their teeth and returned them to their shirt pockets, making sure that the tags dangled outside. They smoked, inhaled deeply, threw their heads back, and blew smoke straight up as they made jokes and stole glances at the girls milling about among older people standing around.

Dick and his young friends arrived. They sat on the bank at the upper side of the church house and played their instruments, taking considerable time to get them in tune. My father arrived about 6:30. He joked with older folk and teased the girls.

The pie mite began with my welcome and my announcement of its purpose. I proposed that all bids for pies begin at twenty-five cents. There would be a guessing contest for five cents a guess, a cake walk at ten cents a couple, and a pie-eating contest at fifty cents a contestant, the winner to receive a cake. My father would cry off the pies and highest bidders would pay me.

Dick and the boys played a lively tune while people gathered in the house. My father, who had a stream of teasing banter, began to cry off the pies, those of little girls first. Pies of little girls were usually bought by their fathers or grandfathers or brothers. Bidding became keen for pies of young women admired by several young men but even keener for the pie of the young woman who had already made her choice of admirers, for groups of young fellows would pool their money to run the price up for the favored one. It was a point of honor to buy the pie of one's own sweetheart at whatever bid that was required.

I was pleased that one pie went for $6.50. After the bidding, the guessing pie was produced. Myrtle Boggs had brought it. It was beautifully decorated. My father smelled it and reported what he thought he could detect. Mostly boys deposited nickels and guessed its filling. After all guesses had been made, Myrtle was called on to announce the filling of her pie. It was boiled peach tree leaves, which produced a most appetizing odor and which one could eat if he wanted to. Those present enjoyed her cleverness but no one claimed the pie.

Fifteen or twenty couples, mostly older folk, entered the cake walk. Seats were pulled together so they could walk around the room. A mark was made on the floor and judges were appointed to choose the winner. Dick and the boys played a slow moving piece that they speeded up considerably before coming to a sudden stop after eight or ten minutes. The couple standing on or judged to be closest to the line on the floor was awarded the cake.

The boys who entered the pie-eating contest were mostly young fellows who had shown no interest in bidding for pies. Some of them were sponsored by their fathers or their sisters' admirers. The winner was the one who had eaten the highest number of quarter of pies in twenty minutes. Ray Williams, then in second grade and sponsored by his father, won the contest, in which the interest of the crowd was lively. He was proud to have the cake.

Following the contest, I announced that we had taken in $31.00 and invited the young men to claim their pies and find the young women who had brought them. They sat around for a half hour, young women holding on their knees the pies in the plates or pans, cutting them with knives they had brought for the purpose, and lifting pieces of them for their admirers. They departed, young men walking beside young women and leading their horses. It was still light enough not to need lanterns or flashlights. I slipped three dollar bills into Dick Sturgill's hand and invited him to spend the night at our house. I had $28.00 for instructional supplies, supplementary readers, and story books.

The following day I made out to A. Flanagan an order that included a set of phonics flash cards, a set of five supplementary readers for first grade, a set of eight supplementary readers for second grade, single copies of story books selected by grade level, a hectograph duplicator, a can of filler for the duplicator, purple ink, special pens, and duplicator paper. On Monday I reported to the school what I had done with our money and explained how it would be possible to provide each student with a set of questions for tests and examinations instead of writing the questions on the blackboard. Many of the titles of the story books, including one volume of biographies of important Americans, had been suggested by students themselves after they had studied the catalog.

The order from A. Flanagan arrived in about ten days. The students were excited by the new books with colorful hard covers. We placed them in the shelf of the organ. Every student in school must have read the first and second readers for the stories and the art work. The story books were checked out and read at home by the older students, many several times by those who liked them especially well.

The first and second graders enjoyed phonics drills. They came to the recitation bench together and responded in unison to each card as it was flashed. Sounding "f," "th," "sh" was so much fun for them that I had to restrain their enthusiasm. After the students had mastered the sounds, I prepared flash cards with words on them to be sounded phonically. Putting the sounds together to build "sixth" and "twelfth" was so fascinating that they would engage in it as a kind of game at play time.

Teaching children to read by the phonics method proved most successful. Every child became a good oral reader. One little boy, not quite five years old at the time the school year began, was reading aloud interpretatively at the third grade level at the end of the year. Enunciation and diction improved remarkably, even among the older students, almost all of whom would stop their studying to witness the performance of the primary children during phonics exercises.

It seemed to me that understanding phonics helped the students in learning to spell orally, for all of them became good spellers, but I required the older students to write their spelling and remained after the close of the school day to check spelling papers, exercises in arithmetic, and written work. The hectograph made it possible for me to supply them with supplementary exercises in arithmetic and language study.

Soon parents began telling me how much their children were enjoying school and how they would report things I had said. The supplementary readers and the exercises I provided by using the hectograph made it possible for the children of extremely poor parents to learn. School was so important to the little children from poor homes that the parents would come with them to help them across the branches and creeks on rainy days. Many of them were so proud of their attendance records that they would come to school, even when they were afflicted with colds and fevers.

In late fall I discovered that I had itch between my fingers. Without saying anything about it, I began to observe the hands of the children and learned that many of them had itch. Remembering unpleasant situations concerning itch and lice from my own school days, I was determined not to allow similar embarrassing accusations and "inspections" to develop in my school. I went to the county health office one Saturday to seek advice. The nurse confirmed that I had itch. She recommended an ointment available at the drugstore for my case and advised that I prescribe the usual sulphur-and-lard treatment for the children.

I bought a large can of the ointment, which I carried to school with me on Monday. After opening exercises I exhibited the can and announced that I had itch. The students laughed loudly. The nurse had prescribed the ointment, I said. I had bought much more than was needed to cure my itch, for I had handled books and papers of the students and had most likely spread itch among them. If so, I wanted them to have some of the medicine too. If they had a "little red breakin' out" like mine between their fingers or on their bodies, they were welcome to a supply of my itch treatment. They could bring from home salve boxes and jars and help themselves. I then told them that they should bathe in as warm water as they could stand, rub themselves vigorously with a towel, apply the ointment, and not change clothes for three days.

I would keep the can of ointment on my desk. If they cared to rub some of it between their fingers during the school day, they were welcome to do so.

The next day several students bought Vick's salve jars and Cloverine salve boxes and filled them with the ointment. Before the week was over, my can was empty. I congratulated myself on handling a sensitive and potentially explosive situation successfully. No parent ever mentioned the incident to me.

One of our topics in health and hygiene was care of the teeth. Most of the students had tooth brushes that they used occasionally but few had toothpaste or powder. They used salt and baking soda instead. I told them that I could get sample tubes of Colgate Dental Cream free and that we might have toothbrush drills at school in order to learn how to brush teeth effectively. They liked the idea. We could brush with water until the samples came. We had already decided that drinking from a common dipper was unsanitary, so everybody had brought a water glass to keep in his desk. But one problem arose. A few children from poor homes did not own toothbrushes. Three pretty little tow-headed sisters told me privately that they would not be able to participate in the drill because they did not own toothbrushes and tried to clean their teeth by rubbing baking soda on them with a "little white rag." Their father did not have money for buying brushes. I asked whether I might go home with them and talk with their father and mother about their problem. They were pleased to have me go.

The following afternoon I went with them to their home, a little unpainted three-room house at the head of the creek. Their father had just come in from work and their mother was preparing supper. Two or three younger tow-headed children were romping about the house and yard, all of them clean and fresh looking.

I told the father that I considered it very important for his children that they participate in the toothbrush drill but that they had said they did not own toothbrushes and that there was no money to buy any. Because I wanted them to be able to participate, I would like to buy each of them a brush if he were willing for me to do so. He looked at the three little girls, each imploring him to consent. He turned and announced through the kitchen door to his wife why I had come. She turned from the stove and came to the door. I repeated that I would like to buy toothbrushes for the children if they were willing for me to do so. The father and mother looked at each other for a moment. Tears came to the mother's eyes as she nodded her head slightly.

The father said he would like for his girls to be able to do what the other children did. They were more interested in school than they had ever been, and they liked me so well for a teacher that they were always saying what I had said as if it was "pure Gospel." Yes, I could buy toothbrushes for them, but he wanted to know what they would cost. He would pay me back when he had the money. I told him that I had not come to urge him to go into debt for the brushes, that I liked his little girls and they were doing so well in school that I wanted to give them the brushes, which would cost ten cents apiece, but that since I did not want to run the risk of hurting his feelings I had thought I ought to talk with him about it.

If I had his permission, I would buy the brushes but they would be gifts and he would owe me nothing.

He was pleased. He and his wife urged that I stay for supper, but I had to go back home and do my share of the evening chores. On the way back I stopped at the country store and post office and bought three toothbrushes, a green one, a blue one, and a red one. Everybody could now participate in the toothbrush drill.

In September I received from the superintendent an announcement of a school field day at Blaine. Teachers of schools around Blaine could bring their students to a field near the school in the village on an appointed Friday to participate in a program of activities that would include singing, recitations, a spelling bee, and such physical contests as sack races, relay races, foot races, broad and high jumping, pole vaulting, rope jumping, and ball games of various kinds.

If such field days had been held while I was student in the one-room school, my teachers had never said anything about them to the students. I believe field days might have been introduced for the first time the year I began teaching. When I announced the field day to the students, they were eager to participate.

We discussed whether it would be possible for all of us to go and what it might cost us to hire the local storekeeper to carry us down to Blaine in his pickup truck. All of the children wanted to go, but they were not certain that their parents would give their permission. That afternoon I walked up to the store and asked the merchant whether he could haul a truck load of the little children for us and what he would charge for doing so. He was willing to take up to about fifteen little ones, who could sit on hay on the bed of the truck, for $2.00.

The following day children reported enthusiastically that parents were willing for them to go but in some cases they would have to walk if it were necessary to pay anything for riding the truck. Larger children were willing to walk or ride horses and mules. I decided that I would pay $2.00 myself and provide transportation free for all of those enrolled in the first three grades and that others could walk or ride horseback. That made it possible for all of them to go. If they cared to take lunches, which could be put in a box in the truck, the trip would not cost them anything. Everybody agreed to go. Although Blaine was only five and a half miles from our school, most of the children had never been there, and some of the little ones had not yet ridden in a car or a truck of any kind.

Field day was going to be exciting, and the children were eager to compete with distinction in the contests. They brought sacks from home for use in practicing for sack races. We determined the winners for each grade each day and decided who our school representatives for each grade would be. We practiced the relay races, foot races, tossing the bean bag, the broad jump and the high jump, and pole vaulting. We identified our best oral spellers, and held speed contests for addition and multiplication. Nobody wanted to sing or give a recitation, but several of the little girls wanted to compete in the rope-skipping contest.

The Friday appointed for the occasion was a bright one. I sat among the little ones in the bed of the truck. They were excited by the speed the driver could make on straight stretches of the dusty road and enjoyed watching the dust boil up and level out behind the truck. They squealed with delight when the driver applied the brakes and they all piled together against the cab. By the time they could disentangle themselves, the driver would shift to second gear and charge up a bank and they would slide with the hay into a heap against the tailgate.

Eight or ten schools came to the field day, many of them in trucks that teachers owned and drove. A teacher selected by the superintendent managed the program, which began with group singing. Contests were then organized for children in the lower grades while older ones went into the school house for the spelling and arithmetic contests. Then all came together on the field again for more singing and the recitations. Big boys competed in pole vaulting, broad jumping, and high jumping and girls in rope-skipping through the lunch period. Following lunch, sack races and other competitions for the older students were held. After the races, teams were selected for a baseball game while judges tallied up scores and prepared to announce winners. Following the baseball game, we sang again, and blue ribbons and honorable mentions were awarded both to individual winners and to the schools from which the highest number of students had won awards. We were pleased to have won second place, for we had outstanding sack runners, racers, and jumpers, but we did not place in spelling or arithmetic. I thought our afternoon exercise program at our school might have conditioned our students for the contests they had entered. We returned to Caines Creek jubilant and happy. The other two schools on the creek had not participated in the activities. Having returned from the field day as winners, we were proud of our achievements and of our school.

About two weeks after the first frost, which came at the end of September in 1929, chestnuts were ripe. It had long been customary at the school to take a Friday afternoon off for chestnut hunting, but in other years children had been permitted to make up their own parties and go in different directions. We decided to go as one group and to hunt hazelnuts and fox grapes as well. We planned our trip along the ridge between the school house branch, called locally Lear Hollow, and the next branch, known as Wolf Hollow, and to dip from the ridge trail down into draws and coves where spreading chestnut trees stood alone in pasture land. Children brought paper pokes and cloth bags from home to hold the pelf they might gather on the hunt.

It was a hazy afternoon with a wind but the hills were bursting with color. Grapes were plump and frosty. Chestnut burs had not yet opened fully, but larger boys and girls, practiced at throwing, were successful in shattering them with sticks and stones. We found only one clump of hazelnut bushes, growing along a ravine below a spring, but there was an ample crop of nuts, their curly and leathery covers still tough. Little children shouted as they raced from one chestnut tree to another to search among the leaves under the trees for satiny nuts before the older children arrived. Before the afternoon was half over, we were all covered with burs—Spanish needles, beggar lice or snatchburs in little strings like beads, cockleburs, which the children called "cuckleburs," waxy nettleburs. Many tripped themselves on sawbriars, but they got up and hurried on without complaining.

After the hunt we returned to the school, counted our chestnuts and hazelnuts, and helped each other scrape the burs from our clothing and pick them from the hair of the little ones. Some of the larger girls had also gathered brilliantly colored leaves with which they decorated the cottage organ.

We had celebrated autumn at the height of the color season and filled our bellies and our pockets with its fruits.

After the entire eighth grade had departed to go to high school, I had only five grades left in the school, first, second, third, fourth, and sixth. The school day began at eight o'clock and closed at four. It was possible for me to complete the checking of papers by five o'clock. Except for three or four hours a week given over to the preparation of flash cards and duplicated materials, I had time for reading in the evenings. I had ordered a catalog from the University of Kentucky and determined that by completing one correspondence course it would be possible for me to meet requirements for a bachelor's degree at the end of the spring semester of 1932-1933 by entering the second semester and continuing through the first summer term.

I ordered a catalog of correspondence courses and selected a course in news writing. The cost was $30.00, for which I was able to write a check from my own account, including most of my salary at $89.00 a month for two pay periods. It was necessary, too, that I purchase a textbook and subscribe to the *New York Times* and one other daily paper. I determined that I would finish the course in three months, so I subscribed to the *Times* and the *Lexington Herald* for three-month periods. The course arrived right away, but the papers did not start coming for about two weeks.

Having been editor of my high school paper during my senior year, I was entertaining the possibility of majoring in journalism at the University and becoming a newspaper writer. Working in the plant of the *Big Sandy News* with Ed Spencer, Earl Kinner, Mrs. MacDougall, Mr. Rankin, and, occasionally, Mr. Milt Conley, who was away most of the time on some kind of a political appointment in Frankfort, had been a pleasant experience for me. I loved the smell of printer's ink, the clatter of the typesetting machine, and the roar and clank of the press. The hurry and bustle in the plant, checking galleys, preparing headlines, and reading excitedly the first copy of the paper off the press had introduced me to a career I might be able to enjoy for a lifetime, it seemed to me. One of the more pleasing aspects of it was the thrill that came from seeing what I had written appear with my by-line in a newspaper column.

I started the correspondence course as soon as the *Times* and the *Herald* began to arrive and tried to complete two or three lessons a week. Since there was much clipping and pasting required for illustrating such things as leads, headlines, straight reporting, human interest stories, and the like, I went to Louisa in Lon McKinnon's bus one Saturday and bought paste, special scissors, a thin ruler, paper clips, construction paper, and other sophisticated materials that would be useful to me in preparing my assignments.

Wanting to profit from comments and suggestions offered by

the teacher, Professor Victor Portmann, I geared the sending of my lessons to the promptness with which lessons I had submitted were returned. Professor Portmann was usually prompt, but if he delayed by two or three weeks his checking and returning lessons, I went right on completing lessons, but double checked them in the light of suggestions on returned lessons before I mailed them to him, sometimes three or four at one mailing. The teacher was generally thorough and painstaking with his comments, criticisms, and commendations, but he rarely assigned me a grade higher than B. Two of his criticisms appeared often: I tended to use too many adjectives, especially adjectives that violated the principle of objective reporting, and my human interest stories were tinged with the sentimental and the romantic. I did best with form, sentence structure, punctuation, and spelling.

I was receiving and reading thoroughly two daily newspapers when the Stock Market Crash in October, 1929, ushered in the Great Depression. I remember standing by the mailbox and reading with a sense of foreboding the *Times* account of Black Thursday as twilight deepened until I could no longer see words clearly enough to complete the stories. Friday's paper arrived the following Monday. Since no one on Caines Creek had a radio with headphones and only one other person in the valley subscribed to a daily newspaper, I was one of the first there to know about the Crash and what it was likely to mean to the national economy if President Hoover should not be able to rescue it. Certainly, hard times lay ahead for people living in cities, but mountain folk living on farms up the creeks and in the coves and who saw little money from year end to year end anyway might not suffer much from the agonies of the ailing economy, it seemed to me. I wrote a paper for the correspondence course based on interviews with my father and his neighbors about the Crash as its effects were expected to ripple their way into the lives of everybody. It seemed so far away and so unrelated to us that my father and his neighbors saw nothing to fear. Having next to no knowledge of economics myself, my own uneasiness about the Crash was relieved somewhat by their confidence in the future.

It seemed important to me that I should attend the annual meeting of the Eastern Kentucky Education Association in Ashland scheduled for the first Thursday, Friday, and Saturday in November. I now had money to dress myself and to buy a good travel "grip" for the occasion. In early October I picked out and ordered a genuine cowhide grip from Sears Roebuck and Company for $9.00. At the same time I ordered three of Sears' best shirts, a tie, some dress socks, and a pair of brown shoes. I was proud of my new blue suit with pencil stripes, but it was really a suit for winter time, I thought, so I ordered also a brown suit with tape-like wine colored stripes, this time without an extra pair of pants, for autumn wear.

My finery arrived in time for me to wear all of it to Ashland. Of course I had a light topcoat, but I would not be likely to need it in early November. I would wait until I had arrived in Lexington to buy a heavy overcoat for winter wear.

I remember that I wore old shoes while walking to Blaine to catch Lon McKinnon's bus and sat on a bank and changed to my new shoes just before I arrived. I felt well groomed when I walked into the Page brothers' barbershop in Louisa for a professional 35-cent haircut before catching a bus for Ashland. I was proud of my new attire and the good-looking tan traveling bag that I set against the wall while waiting for my turn for a haircut. The plaid cap with a cork bill I had worn since my senior year in high school was still a good and handsome one, but I would buy myself a snappy tan Adam hat with a dark brown band after I reached Ashland. I would then be dressed from top to toe in new clothes that not only caught the spirit of autumn but also compensated my ego for the shame of having had to wear shabby clothes to the teachers institute in July.

I walked up to John Garred's restaurant for lunch, proud that I had enough money in my pocket to sit at a table in a restaurant and order a lunch from a menu, meat, two vegetables, and a drink for 35 cents. I am sure I left no tip for the red-haired girl who waited on me, for I do not believe I knew then that leaving a tip was expected.

The bus to Ashland was crowded with teachers on their way to the meeting, but I knew only two or three of them. I sat beside someone who appeared to be from Johnson County from what I could pick up from his conversation with a couple occupying the seats in front of us. He never spoke to me, nor did either of those from the seat in front of us. I sat in stony silence, as if I were not hearing what they were saying.

The bus station in Ashland at that time was located beside the back entrance to the Arcade. I had not reserved a room at a hotel, for I did not know that one could do so. I slipped my plaid cap into my handy grip and walked proudly through the Arcade to Winchester Avenue, my leather heels tapping the tile, the new leather in the handle of my grip creaking richly in response to the rhythm of my steps, and the faint odor of the tonic Ben Page had splashed on my hair circling my face. I crossed Winchester Avenue and made my way down the left side of the street toward Greenup Avenue, where I saw a sign for a small hotel, Savoy, as I recall. There was one single room available. The price was $3.00. The room had a wash basin in it, but the bathroom was down the hall. This did not disturb me, for I had not yet learned that it was possible to rent a hotel room with a bathroom in it. The room seemed to be clean, but I could smell the odor of stale cigar smoke hanging about, the wash basin was old and cracked, and the towels on the rack, though clean, were worn and ragged at the edges.

I left my grip in the room and went to buy a hat and a writing pad for taking notes on lectures that I could use in writing news reports of public lectures for my correspondence course. I found a hat shop for men near the Henry Clay Hotel, the headquarters for the EKEA meeting. I was handed a printed program and a map of downtown Ashland on which churches and hotels in which meetings were scheduled were identified.

I did not see many people whom I had known at the meeting. Apparently most of the teachers from around Blaine had chosen not to come, but I recognized a few from Louisa and up and down the Mayo Trail. The first general session of the association was scheduled for a church auditorium that evening.

That evening I ate my dinner in a crowded restaurant on the north side of Winchester Avenue. Being alone, I sat at the counter, but I noticed that few dressed-up people were eating there. Men in work clothes sat crowded around tables in the dimly lighted place, and overweight waitresses in soiled white dresses, all looking alike, hurried among the tables. After dinner I strolled up and down the avenue and back and forth through the Arcade studying displays in windows and reading signs that welcomed EKEA. I finally decided that probably most of the teachers were milling around registration headquarters at the Henry Clay Hotel and that I might meet someone there whom I had known and with whom I could walk to the church for the first session.

Just as I was ready to enter the hotel lobby, I met Dock Jordan, our superintendent. He was most cordial and genuinely pleased, it seemed to me, that I had come to the meeting. While we were talking, two of the older teachers from Lawrence County walked up and entered the conversation. As we moved to take leave of one another, Dock Jordan asked one of the older men to lend him $2.00. Dock had forgotten to go by the bank before he left Louisa, he said, and discovered after he arrived in Ashland that he did not have enough money in his pocket to buy his meals after holding back enough to pay for his hotel room. I was impressed by his open, unabashed candor while thinking that I probably would have eaten peanuts and apples instead of asking to borrow money.

I met no one whom I had known, so I studied the map and found my way to the church. There must have been five or six hundred teachers present at the first session of EKEA. The auditorium was dark, but the stage was well lighted. I found a seat near the back. It was too dark for me to take notes on the speech made by the new president of Morehead State Teachers College, but I was fascinated by his oratorical style and his gestures. I do not remember the title of his speech nor any of the content, but I recall that he closed it with a dramatic recitation of Joaquin Miller's "Columbus," the poem I had recited the first time I ever appeared before an audience.

The only speech I was able to take notes on during the meeting was delivered by a white-haired psychologist from Ohio State University in that same church on Saturday morning. That meeting had not attracted many of the teachers, perhaps not more than a hundred. Light filtered through the stained glass windows and the lighting around the pulpit where the speaker stood was subdued. I sat at the end of a bench about a third of the way from the front. I do not remember the professor's topic nor anything he said, but he delivered a well organized speech in a calm voice and used no gestures at all. It was easy for me to take notes.

No one else in the audience appeared to be taking notes. After a while it seemed to me that the speaker was addressing himself to me. When I looked at him, he was looking at me. At first I felt self-conscious and wondered whether it was appropriate for me to be taking notes, but I was supposed to prepare a story on a public lecture and this lecture would be the only one I would have an opportunity to take notes on. In my confusion I stole a glance to my right. Several people within the arc of my glance were looking at me, too. As I was turning my face back toward the speaker, I noticed two young women sitting half way across on the bench on which I was sitting. The blond one, sitting nearer me, presented a fine profile, erect and dignified, but a slight smile on her face led me to believe that she had most likely turned away immediately before my glance fell upon her. The other, with dark hair, wide eyes, and a free smile, was bent forward and looking directly at me as if she were most curious as to why I might be taking notes. I concentrated my attention on my note taking, but when I would look up at the speaker, he was looking at me.

I stole another quick glance at the young women. The blond one, obviously not wanting me to discover her looking at me, quickly presented her profile again. It was then that I recognized them as the two young women who had sat by the window at the teachers institute in the courthouse in July. They were Lawrence County teachers, but I did not know their names. They were exceptionally well dressed, it seemed to me, and had no doubt come to the meeting determined to take it all in, since they were among the small Saturday morning audience. My knowing that they were watching me take notes made me uncomfortable. I was enjoying the speech, the speaker, I realized by then, was relating to me, possibly because he needed the assurance that he was communicating with somebody in that large room with most of his small audience, like Baptists at church, sitting on the back rows so far away from him that their faces must have looked like blanks, and I was relating to the speaker with an unusual interest in what he was saying. But those two young women seemed to be more amused at me than they were interested in the speaker. I wished they would look the other way, or go to sleep, or something.

Following that session I hurried back to the hotel, paid my bill, stopped at a diner for a sandwich, walked to the bus station, and bought my ticket. The station was crowded. Many people were standing around, some looking at post cards on a rack, some picking up magazines and looking at them for a moment and returning them to their place, and some leaning against the wall, their bags and suitcases with coats folded across them beside them on the floor. I stood near the door and looked at the people to see whether there were any I knew. Side by side in seats at the back of the station sat the two young women who had been amused by my note taking, one reading a magazine and the other writing on a sheet of paper she was holding on a book that rested on her knee. They seemed completely oblivious of all the others who were waiting for their bus.

In addition to teachers, many men who worked in Ashland but lived along the Mayo Trail and women who had come to town to shop at the department stores were waiting on the landing to board the bus. I was able to find a place in the overhead baggage rack for my grip but stood in the aisle for a few miles beyond Cannonsburg. Conversation was lively among the working men, but teachers and women with paper bags on their laps sat silently and stared out the windows at the passing countryside. The afternoon was cloudy. The hills, though it was not yet mid November, had little of autumn left on them and were dark behind a shimmer of thin mist. I was able to take a seat by a fat man who was smoking a cigar, perhaps a salesman on his way home for Saturday night and Sunday. He did not look at me as I sank into the seat beside him and we did not greet each other.

The bus was warm. My vested brown suit of worsted wool was too warm in the crowded bus. Soon I was dozing, the monotony of the voices around me articulating itself in my dreams as a conversation about the psychology of learning that I was enjoying with the white-haired professor whose lecture I had heard that morning. Occasionally I would wake up enough to recognize that the last of a sentence I heard rising above the babble of voices could not be the end of the sentence I had dreamed, but I could not by then remember the beginning of the sentence from my dream.

Perhaps I should write down what the professor was saying. I dreamed beautiful sentences that Professor Portmann would like in the news story I was to write, but by the time I had thought through them, I could not remember how they had begun.

As we approached Louisa, people waiting by the roadside were getting on the bus. I would wake up enough to see them close their umbrellas as they entered. They stood in the aisles and propped themselves against seats with their folded umbrellas planted firmly on the floor. In Louisa most of the riders disembarked, some leaving hats or packages on seats that they would claim after a rest stop at Atkins and Vaughan's Drug Store, in which the bus station was located. I found my grip and got off, noting that my seatmate, who was remaining on the bus, was staring out the window.

Lon McKinnon's bus had already left for Blaine. He would not make another trip that afternoon. He would leave for Blaine on Sunday at one o'clock.

I walked through a light rain to the courthouse to use the restroom and wash my face. Then I walked down to Sac Pigg's boardinghouse two blocks away and engaged a room for the night. It was a small room that one entered from the second floor of the porch. Someone might be assigned to the room with me. The price was $1.50. If I cared to eat dinner at the boardinghouse, that would be 50 cents extra, and the breakfast would cost 25 cents. I made a reservation for breakfast but said that I would eat dinner with friends up the street. I lit the tiny gas stove and stood near it to dry the moisture from my clothes. Dry and warm, I found the bathroom, where I brushed my teeth and rubbed shaving lotion on my face even though I had not shaved that day, combed my hair, and arranged my tie.

With my new Adam hat cocked at a jaunty angle over my right eye, I stood on the second floor of the porch and waited for the shower to stop. After a time the rain slowed to a light drizzle and I walked up to the drug store. Young people were gathering there, but those I recognized had been sophomores in high school the year I had graduated. They were seniors this year, grown now out of their awkward age and many of them eighteen, my age. Two young men in a booth, Kenneth Hayes and John Skaggs, invited me to sit with them. Peggy Wellman, the waitress, who had always worn beautiful make-up and pretty clothes and who looked just the same as I remembered her, came to take my order. I called for a Coca-Cola and asked the young men whether they were ready for another drink. They were. I was inwardly pleased to remember that I had never before sat with young men and been financially able to offer to buy drinks for them as I counted out 30 cents. Either we did not leave tips then or I did not know a tip was expected.

John and Kenneth, apparently still shy about girls, talked about escapades they had been engaged in at the high school, their most recent one a trick they had rigged up to ring the bell at the top of the high tower by tying a second rope to it, pulling the rope through a hole into the attic above the auditorium, and ringing the bell from the dark corner of the attic. When Mr. Ellis, the principal, rushed out to see what was happening, he found the regular bell rope dancing in the tower while the bell rang lustily, apparently of its own volition. Students were rushing to their next classes, many of them not aware that the bell was ringing ahead of schedule. John and Kenneth had been able to ring the bell early several times over a period of four or five days before the principal discovered what had happened, but he never knew that they had been the mischief makers. They recalled and elaborated upon tricks others had played: pouring vials of hydrogen sulfide on the floor of the auditorium while local preachers prayed at student assemblies, throwing stink bombs against the wall in study hall, stealing frogs preserved with formaldehyde from the science laboratory and hiding them in the pockets of the overcoats of the young fellows who were the Beau

Brummells at the school, pouring sulphuric acid in the side pocket of Mr. Gilmer's pants while some young woman was asking him questions about the experiment she was performing at her work desk, arranging dates with girls for young men who were to meet them at the lumber yard and then hiding to watch the young men wait for the girls who knew nothing about the arrangement, stalking the unmarried teachers on their dates in cars with the eligible bachelors in town, concealing condoms in the textbooks of old maid teachers so they would fall out when the teachers opened their books before their classes, rubbing fresh cat manure on the door handles of cars that unmarried young men teachers drove.

Many of the tricks had been perpetrated while I was a student at the school. Accounts of them were living and growing in the lore of the students. Kenneth and John were passing them along as if the fabric of mischief that has taken place at a school is one of its more becoming garments, the stories comprising one aspect of the life of a school that gives it uniqueness, that makes it a school one can be proud to have attended.

I was aware of their provincialism and slightly dampened by their lack of interest in what I might have been doing since I graduated from high school. That I had gone to college a year and was now teaching school satisfied them. I did not feel free to tell them about college, the long, hard hours one must spend in preparation for classes and examinations, the writing of papers about books one has read. Real college life was not what one found in the popular magazines and movies. Joe College had not been a student at Cumberland. Perhaps he was enrolled at Harvard, or Yale, or Princeton, but not at Cumberland, where not even one student owned a coonskin coat. I was proud of my school on Caines Creek and could have talked about the things I was doing there, but I felt that they would not be interested in what goes on in a one-room country school.

Peggy came by to pick up our glasses. When she asked whether we wanted anything else, I ordered another Coca-Cola and invited John and Kenneth to have one. They ordered another also, and I counted down thirty cents. It was raining outside. People coming in now were dressed in brightly colored slickers and rainhats. Slender little girls with pipestem legs whom I had known two years earlier were now fleshed out, their shapely legs sheathed in flesh-colored hose rolled below their knees, their short skirts coming only two-thirds of the way down their rouged thighs, their eyebrows thin dark arches above their eyes, deep pools behind lashes darkened with mascara, their cheeks rouged, and their lips bright red Cupid bows drawn back around flashing teeth. Eyes straight ahead and chins tilted, they passed our booth, trailing the odor of oilskin slickers and perfume as the slickers rattled from the stiffness produced by the cold rain outside. No one appeared to recognize me, though I was sitting on the outside and facing them as they made their way to seats at little round tables and in booths behind me.

I began to feel that I was older than those around me, even though I knew many of them were also eighteen. Something had happened to me. I had grown beyond John and Kenneth, both much larger and more mature looking than I and about my age. The girls, pretty, well groomed, smelling good, all looked alike, sitting around the little tables and flashing their legs and staring in silence behind their uneasy masks of boredom as they sipped their sodas through straws so slowly that I wondered whether perhaps they had brought only one dime each in their shining compacts and wanted to make their sodas last as long as they would. One by one, they opened their compacts, held them on the table tops, and freshened their make-up and patted down the curls arranged around their foreheads. Kenneth and John, paying no attention to the girls, continued to regale me with accounts of escapades and how many students "got by with murder" in what they wrote in their laboratory books for Mr. Gilmer. One boy had written the Lord's Prayer, the Twenty-Third Psalm, the Pledge of Allegiance, the Declaration of Independence, and Lincoln's "Gettysburg Address" in his book, but the young woman who helped Mr. Gilmer evaluate the books had promised him that she would simply report that he had written full accounts of all of the experiments he had performed. Mr. Gilmer had not called for the book to be spot read through his magnifying glass as he was accustomed to doing for students whose laboratory work seemed less than satisfactory to him.

After finishing our drinks, we left the drug store. The rain had stopped and a cool wind was blowing. John and Kenneth went home for their suppers. I walked with John to the railroad station, where people who had done their shopping were waiting for the "down train," not due for another hour or more. I sat for a while on one of the hard benches and warmed myself by the gas stove in the dimly lighted room. Women sat in silence beside bundles and shopping bags while the telegraphs clicked in Morse code and men standing in clusters under the shed outside the open door laughed loudly at one another's jokes and yarns.

Having dozed for a few minutes before the gas stove, I got up and walked down the platform to a restaurant beside the railroad tracks for dinner. Those sitting at the tables and in the booths I recognized as persons I had seen delivering laundry and dry cleaning, working in yards, sweeping floors in the business buildings, cleaning the streets, or loading and unloading at the hardware stores and the wholesale houses while I was in high school. I sat at the counter and ordered a 35-cent dinner consisting of quite hard hamburger patties, thin mashed potatoes, overcooked navy beans, limp slaw, biscuits with too much baking powder in them, Nehi grape soda, and a small serving of peach cobbler that contained very little peach in a soggy mixture that had not been cooked long enough. I think I might have begun developing discrimination in the selection of eateries at that restaurant, which was operated by a hollow-eyed older man, his fat wife with buns under her hairnet and flour and grease on her apron, and their slab-sided old maid daughter who served as the waitress and dispensed cheer, with her giggle and her teasing high-pitched comments, as she hurried about among the laughing men who wolfed down their food as they called for more biscuits and coffee. These men, who would have felt uncomfortable at John Garred's Restaurant, were relaxed and happy here where they felt they "got their money's worth" in the platefuls of sloppy food, the seconds of baking powder biscuits, and the refills of coffee that had boiled all day on grounds that had been accumulating in the big pot since last Sunday.

After dinner I walked back to the drug store, stood against the front, and watched people in raincoats parade by until time for the first show at the Garden Theatre. Mrs. Tillman, who had always sold me a child's ticket for a dime while I was in high school, smiled but said nothing to indicate that she recognized me when I counted out thirty cents and called for one adult ticket. I do not remember the "western" shown that night, but I enjoyed the popular music played on the piano by Edith Adams, who played while the crowd was gathering. Talking movies had not yet arrived at the Garden Theatre. Little Frank Kirk in his wheelchair was continuing to operate his hot popcorn concession at the entrance to the theatre.

After the show I stopped at the drug store again. Seats were taken, but I ordered a Coca-Cola and stood by the counter to sip it. George Burgess and Junior Lackey, whom I had known, sat with Ellen Lackey at one of the little tables. They invited me over for a brief conversation, in which they congratulated me for having finished a year of college, asked about my plans for the future, and encouraged me to complete my college education at the University of Kentucky.

Back at the boardinghouse I was invited to come into the living room and sit for a while with Aunt Sac Pigg's family, which at the time included her widowed daughter and her two grandchildren, Fred and Lelia Braid. Fred Braid, two or three years behind me in high school, invited me into his room to listen to his own radio, an up-to-date one that did not require the listener to wear earphones. Other young fellows came during the evening to listen to the programs, which Fred was proud to be able to "turn up loud" on his new radio. We were so fascinated by the performance of the set that we conversed very little.

I retired to my room about eleven o'clock, turned off the little gas stove, opened the window two or three inches for fresh air, and went to sleep, but I experienced during the night a sense of homecoming to Louisa as the long freight trains rumbled up and down the Big Sandy Valley, the Norfolk and Western on the West Virginia side of the river and the Chesapeake and Ohio on the Kentucky side. The long, lonesome calls of the locomotives in the night and the rattle of the wheels on the tracks echoed and reverberated among the low hills in a pattern that had become a part of the way I experienced the town during the four and a half years I had gone to school there.

Sunday morning was dark and drizzly. After breakfast, which I ate alone at a corner of the big dining table, I returned to my room and wrote my news story covering the "public lecture" of the white-haired psychology professor. Had the weather been more pleasant, I might have enjoyed going to church, but I had not brought my yellow slicker with me on my trip and I did not want to risk getting my new brown suit wet. The day became brighter about 11:30 and the rain stopped. I packed my little grip, paid my bill, and walked up to the main street, where I stopped for a hamburger at Rip's stand, a tiny little place jammed between Justice's Department Store and the Savoy Hotel. One ordered a hamburger at Rip's at a counter beside the sidewalk, stood by the counter, and watched the cook fry it while the odors of the frying meat, the freshly sliced onion, and the mustard assaulted him. He then stood by the counter or at the edge of the street and ate it, while washing it down with soda or Coca-Cola. By then, Rip was so well known for the quality of his hamburgers that his customers repeated with emphasis his slogan, "Hamburgers that am burgers!"

Lon McKinnon was ready to leave for Blaine at one o'clock. The sky was overcast but the rain had stopped. There had been enough rainfall to lay the dust in the roads but not enough to make them muddy except in the low places beyond the end of the still ungraveled new highway. It was being built slowly toward Blaine and ultimately to Sandy Hook in Elliott County, a highway link in the county-seat-to-seat program that Kentucky had begun eight or nine years earlier. Lon McKinnon had only three passengers to Blaine that afternoon, the other two of whom, an older couple returning for a visit with kinfolk, sat in silence on the back seat.

As soon as I was out of sight of people at Blaine, I stopped, changed from my new shoes to the old ones in my grip, rolled up the legs of my pants so I would not get mud on them, and struck the "mountain lope" for Caines Creek. I felt good about my first attendance at a professional meeting. I had not felt unworthy or inadequate in any sense but I continued to feel uneasy about the appropriateness of my taking notes at the lecture, with the lecturer himself concentrating his attention upon me while everybody seated near stared. But I was pleased to have heard a real public lecture for reporting in the news story I had written that morning.

While walking the muddy road up Caines Creek that cloudy Sunday afternoon, I saw no one at the house from whose chimneys thin columns of smoke were rising, and I met only two people, boys riding horseback and double an old mule with a blind bridle on. I thought they were the sons of Meredith Edwards, who lived on Deans Branch and from whom my father bought his supply of coal each year.

No other teacher from the Blaine section had gone to the meeting of the educational association. I would receive pay for the two days I had taken off to go. The trip had cost me more than I would receive for the two days, but I was pleased that I had taken it. I felt more professional for the experience and would go again next year if it were possible for me to do so. Owning a car would make such trips much easier for me and would enable me to drive to Blaine and Louisa when I wanted to go there, but I could not consider owning one until after I had finished my college program.

Our school had never had a Christmas tree. I proposed one. We could draw names for little gifts not to cost more than a nickel if bought at the store or the gifts could be cookies, homemade candy or taffy, apples from the hole, or any little thing one might care to make for a gift, like a whistle from a branch of a buckeye tree, a jimmy-dancer whittled from a spool, a popgun made from an alder bush trunk, a doll made from a corncob, a monkey-on-a-string whittled from an old shingle, a cornstalk fiddle, a slingshot, cutouts colored with crayons I had bought with pie mite money. For the tree to have meaning, everybody should want to give something. If the children should be interested, they could talk with their parents about it and we would then decide whether we should attempt to have one.

Interest in a Christmas tree was keen. Everybody wanted to participate. We discussed how the tree should be decorated. Children brought colored pictures of Christmas trees they found in Sears Roebuck and Montgomery Ward catalogs. We could not have candles on our tree or lights of any kind, but we could decorate it with whatever we thought we could create that would help make it festive.

Girls strung popcorn on threads. Boys gathered red haws, wahoo berries, wild rose apples for the girls to thread. Children collected tinfoil for wrapping sycamore and swamp wood balls to hang on the tree. Someone brought sage apples to have on it. Colored pictures of Santa Claus were pasted to cardboard. Sticks of wood and cuttings from stickweeds were wrapped with twists of paper. Red bells were made from crepe paper. Imitation candles with yellow flamelike flags pinned in the top were anchored to cardboard discs to be placed here and there on the tree. A cardboard cylinder with a star covered with tinfoil was prepared for the top of the tree. Gold and silver glass beads as big as marbles dangled at the ends of knotted strings to be tied to twigs. One of the boys had his father help him make a base for the tree, a cross of wood with angle supports. The cross could be nailed to the floor and the angle supports to the tree from four directions.

We received from Jay Boggs, who owned the land around the school, permission to cut an evergreen tree, a small cedar if we could find one. A week before Christmas Eve, we found and set up a cedar tree about five feet tall, and the children began to decorate it. So much decoration was needed, though, that they decided to decorate only two-thirds of its circumference, since no one would be seeing the third of it turned toward the corner of the room. One of the girls brought a bedsheet to go around the base of the tree and spread outward for presents that seemed too big or awkwardly shaped to hang on limbs.

We would have a Santa Claus. We did not have a red suit for Santa, but I had a Santa Claus beard that could be worn with a red pullover cap. We would want Santa to wear boots, around which we could tie strips of white and red cloth.

Then we planned a program to include recitations of poems about Christmas that we had in our readers and the biblical account of the birth of the Christ child in the manger. I would ask Dick Sturgill to bring his fiddle and play music for us and to be Santa Claus. Parents, children at home, and grandparents could come. I would buy some stick candy, mixed candy, and jelly beans to distribute after Santa had given out the gifts. We selected two third grade boys to be Santa's helpers. We would have our Christmas program at ten o'clock on Christmas Eve day and dismiss school when the program was over.

Although Christmas Eve day was warm, the roads were muddy, and a light rain was falling, everybody came to school that day. Mothers and fathers carrying children too little to walk came along with younger pupils, many of them followed by the family dogs, who came inside and sat beside their owners.

Dick Sturgill was there with his fiddle, but he had not worn either rubber boots or a red pullover cap. He agreed to wear a cap of one of the children and for the girls to tie the strips of red and white cloth over his pants and around his legs just below his knees.

We first had the program of readings and recitations, including Moore's "A Visit from St. Nicholas," then some fiddling, and then, while Dick was in the cloakroom permitting himself to be dressed as Santa Claus, some singing of Christmas songs and patriotic songs. Dick then appeared as Santa Claus, his red false face with the manila fiber beard somewhat askew because he had not pulled his cap on evenly. But the children squealed gleefully and the little ones in their mother's arms withdrew from him as he attempted to pat them on the head while making his way to the tree at the front of the room.

He had a delightful patter that included an appreciation of the tree, its pretty decorations, how good children are, especially just before Christmas when they are as good as they can be. He called for his helpers, one to find the gifts on and under the tree and present them to him and another to deliver them to the good children present. The children were surprised, delighted, and happy as they tore away from the brown paper wrappings secured by pieces of string, some torn from strips of old cloth, to find what they were receiving. Some got packs of chewing gum, some bars of candy, little bags of homemade cookies, or candy, or a shining red apple, or a little toy carefully whittled out with a sharp pocket knife.

I then asked Santa's helpers to place a page torn from a Sears Roebuck catalog on the desk before each person in the room, broke open the packages of candy I had bought, and had the helper lay a piece on each catalog page until the candy had all been distributed. As I recall, each received a total of five pieces of candy.

I thanked the parents, grandparents, and little ones for coming, hoped that Santa Claus might find each stocking hung with care on the backs of chairs that night, and wished them all a Merry Christmas.

Thereafter, people in the valley began to have Christmas trees at home for the little children and to save pretty baubles in shoe boxes hidden away in attics and closets and safes from one year to the next to decorate them with.

One-room country schools closed only for Christmas Day and New Year's Day, but people were in a holiday mood for the twelve days of Christmas. Children brought to school with them during that season pieces of stack cake (called "fruit cake" locally) in their lunch buckets, gingerbread cookies, pieces of cake decorated with cinnamon hearts, cinnamon bark that they chewed secretly during the school day, pieces of brown paper pokes soaked in cinnamon oil that they chewed like chewing gum, and shining red apples that they ate at recess. New sweaters, cotton gloves, caps, brightly colored stockings were worn with pride. During that season young people of courting age met at homes for parties at which they made taffy from sorghum molasses, "sea foam" and fudge candy, and popcorn balls and played games like "Going Out West," "Post Office," "Climbing the Cherry Tree," and "Bottoming the Sled." Young women carried with them their newest 78 rpm records of favorite country music stars. Admiring young men stood close by the photographs to keep them wound up. During that time, too, housewives, their heads wrapped with new fascinators, the ends of which whipped in the wind, carried baskets of eggs along the muddy roads to the store to exchange for staples needed for Christmas cooking and for little "extras" for the youngens. Men rode horses or mules over the community and visited one another, some carrying flasks of whiskey concealed in flapping saddlebags or inside coat pockets. They had drawn the whiskey from charred kegs in which their year's supply had been aging since late summer. Grandparents, often toward the end of the season, would visit among their children, dispensing from the depths of heavy coats red apples, nuts, and such little "play purties" as brightly colored bottles, tin boxes, or cartons that they had been saving.

I attended one memorable party at Arb Gambill's during the season. The eighth graders who had entered high school in September were all there as well as others of courting age from the district. Young people of high school age from other communities also came. The ground, frozen hard, was covered with a light snow, and the moon was full and bright. The party had continued to midnight, but one of the more pleasant aspects of the affair was the singing and the cutting of capers we enjoyed as we walked down the frozen road from the Gambill home. Among the happiest was my sister, who had returned for the holidays from Morehead State Teachers College, where she was a student in the Breckinridge Training School.

Attendance at school dropped sharply after New Year's Day. Rough weather, snow and ice, muddy roads kept smaller children who lived far from school at home. It was too cold for play outside the school building during most of January, but we continued to do our exercises morning and afternoon beside the seats. At recess periods and the noon hour we played blindfold, puss in the corner, pin the tail on the donkey, and bean bag. Some days the games would become so lively that the children would perspire and the room would be filled with the odors of homemade soap and perspiration steaming from their clothing.

As the end of the school year approached, we prepared for final examinations. It was possible for me to supply long lists of review questions in history, civics, geography, health, and language by writing the questions and preparing multiple copies with the hectograph. They worked together to find answers and drilled each other in review periods. We reviewed spelling, both by spelling matches and by writing lists of twenty words at a time. We had adding matches, contests in subtraction and long division, and drills in multiplication at the blackboard. Better students worked with slower students to help them improve their skills.

Next to the last day was set aside for examinations. All day students wrote, including the first graders who were by then able to read simple questions to which they could write answers, write spelling lists, do simple sums in arithmetic. Everybody was pleased to have his own set of questions on his desk before him. I spent the day grading papers and recording grades in the big record book. That night I finished papers in history and geography and completed the averaging of grades in the record book.

Early on the last day I went to the store and bought five one-pound boxes of stick candy for the teacher's treat. It was a cloudy day and the roads had thawed, so most of those who had not been able to attend school in January were able to come for the teacher's last-day treat. Everybody was dressed in his best. Little children looked eagerly at the stack of square boxes of candy on the desk.

Examination papers were returned. I read off the names of those who were to be promoted to the next grade, which included all of the children who had taken the examinations. I then gave perfect attendance awards of 50 cents each to thirteen of the twenty-seven left after the eighth graders had gone on to high school. Lesser amounts were awarded the best speller in school and the best in arithmetic. An award was given also to each student who had made a perfect record in health habits, including washing hands and face, combing the hair and brushing the teeth each day and taking a bath at least once each week.

I then laid on a piece of paper on each child's desk sticks of candy from the five boxes, some peppermint, some horehound, some sassafras, some lemon, until the boxes were empty.

Many of the children were sad that the school was ending. All thought we had had a good school. They were proud that it had not been necessary for me to whip anybody for misbehavior. Only a few times had I asked a student to stand in the corner or beside his desk for a few minutes to think about his behavior as it affected others. All hoped that I might return to teach the school the following year.

That afternoon I finished filling out the record book, completed the monthly attendance report, and mailed the book and the report to the superintendents's office. I had completed my first year of teaching before my nineteenth birthday.

Two experiences that first year made deep and lasting impressions on me.

One bright little boy, the youngest in his family and the favorite of his father, had a speech impediment. He talked so fast that it was difficult to understand what he was saying. Other children mimicked him playfully, and asked him to say again for their amusement things that sounded funny to them. Everybody stopped studying to listen to him read aloud and laughed when he mispronounced words. I observed that the boy was having difficulty with palatals. He said "sty" and "tloud" for "sky" and "cloud," "drampa" for "grandpa," and his "l" and "r" did not come out for certain vowels, especially when they were related to nasals. He said, "borne" for "barn," "forme" for "farm." One day I asked him at recess when no one was close by to pronounce words after me. He was unable to pronounce them correctly. I then asked if he would let me look in his mouth. He opened his mouth widely and I squatted in front of him to look into it. He had the steepest, highest palate I had ever seen. It was so high that the boy's tongue simply did not make contact with it when he tried to say "cloud."

I worked with him carefully for a few minutes a day for a week or two and taught him how to slow down and take the time to lift his tongue to his palate to be sure the sounds were formed correctly. He was so proud of his achievements that his speech became almost normal within a few weeks, although a hissing continued with certain sounds until he was grown. It occurred to me that his grandfather, then an old man with a white beard, and his uncle, then approaching middle age, had similar speech impediments. No doubt the steep palate was an inherited trait, but apparently nobody had ever attempted to help the grandfather and the uncle to overcome the difficulty.

Paul Alexander, the teacher at Upper Caines Creek School, married Christine Ison, one of the young women in the district who had tired of repeating eighth grade but had not cared to go to the new high school at Blaine. I attended the wedding, to which Christine's nieces, whose fathers were coal miners in Pike County, came. One of the nieces, tall, slender, black haired, and with almost violet eyes in a beautiful face, attracted my attention. I sat with her in the porch swing for a time after the wedding. We liked each other. She would return to Pike County the following day with her parents, but they would come back for a visit in a few weeks. She would be glad to have me come to see her when she came back. I got her name, Irene Miller, and her address, McVeigh, Kentucky. We exchanged letters.

When she came back to visit her grandmother, I had dates with her in the evening. Following a long date from which I returned about two o'clock in the morning, I was tired and sleepy next day.

Everything went wrong at school. I was irritable. The children had little interest in what they were doing. The school almost deteriorated into a pandemonium while I fussed and scowled. My temper was bad. The one day when they should have been especially good the children were particularly trying on my nerves. My speaking sharply to them had seemed to make them worse. On my way home that afternoon I recognized that that day had been the only day all year that I had not enjoyed. It occurred to me that the trouble was mine, not the children's. My own feelings, the state of my irritability, my private problems, must not in any way affect my attitude and behavior as a teacher. A teacher, when before the class, is a public person. A public person does not betray in attitude or behavior his private feelings. That was one of the soundest principles I ever learned in my life. I have been amazed at the numbers of teachers, secretaries, and administrators I have known, many of them with years of experience, who never had learned that lesson.

Cratis D. Williams
1978

MSU Photo.

Two Autobiographical Statements

About the Author

A Narrative Vita

Cratis Williams,[1] born April 5, 1911, on Caines Creek near the village of Blaine in Lawrence County, Kentucky, was the oldest of the five children of Curtis and Mona Whitt Williams. Mostly of Scotch-Irish origin, his ancestors living at that time were all on the Appalachian frontier when our nation was founded. Among his forebears were Indian fighters, long hunters, veterans of the American Revolution, Tories escaped to the backwoods, refugees from the Whiskey Rebellion, Kentucky mountain feudists, and religious dissenters. He thinks of himself as a "complete mountaineer."

As he was growing up, Caines Creek, best known for its many family distilleries and renowned for the quality of their product, remained isolated and relatively untouched by influences from the outside. He learned the traditions of his people, whose music, dances, songs, hymns, religious attitudes, manners, customs, folkways, and speech were essentially those of the pioneers of the 18th century.

He attended Hillside School, known also as Middle Caines Creek, a one-room school held in the Caines Creek United Baptist Church, which had the largest membership of the churches in the Blaine Association of United Baptists. After he had passed a two-day examination for admission to high school, his father took him to Louisa in 1924 and enrolled him in the high school there. He was the first from Caines Creek to graduate from a high school.

At first painfully ashamed of the quaint background he brought directly into the glitter of the Jazz Age with its flappers and candy-ankles which had arrived in Louisa ahead of him, he soon adjusted to his new surroundings. He became interested in the traditional English and Scottish ballads when he learned that the texts in his high school literature book differed from those still being sung by his kin and their neighbors back in the hills 25 miles from Louisa. He began as a high school youngster to collect and learn traditional and native ballads, songs, and hymns exactly as they were sung by his people and to study the speech, tales, and oral rhetoric of mountain folk.

A serious student and active in debate, declamation, and drama, Cratis Williams became in his senior year the editor of the *Louisian*, the five-column four-page school newspaper published twice a month and printed by the *Big Sandy News*. While seeing the paper through presses, he became acquainted with the publisher, Milt Conley, and with Ed Spencer and Earl Kinner, who were working for the *News* then. At the high school commencement in 1928, when he delivered the salutatory address, Williams was the recipient of the honor student award, an 18-inch silver loving cup given by the faculty to the graduate who best exemplified scholarship and leadership.

Through the help of his principal, William H. Vaughan, Cratis Williams was awarded a tuition scholarship and a workship by Cumberland College at Williamsburg. After a year at Cumberland, he became a one-room school teacher on Caines Creek in 1929 and continued with his college education by attending the second semester and one summer term each year at the University of Kentucky. He received the A.B. degree in June 1933.

In 1933 Williams became the science teacher at Blaine High School, where he continued as the English teacher and principal from

Cratis Williams—age sixteen.
Courtesy of the Williams Family Collection.

1934 to 1938. While working there, he completed requirements in 1937 for the M.A. degree in English at the University of Kentucky.

His master's thesis, written on the ballads and songs of Eastern Kentucky, has been published on microcard for the use of scholars in folklore. His thesis was used extensively by Malcolm Laws in his revised edition of *Native American Balladry*. As Williams grew older, his interest turned to the total tradition of what he thought at the time was the dying culture of the Appalachian mountaineers. His dissertation, called by a writer for the *Journal of American Folklore* "the most comprehensive and valuable current work on Southern Highland literature," was written on the Southern Mountaineer in fact and fiction. The product of eight years of research and writing, the 1,600-page document, which examines the social and cultural history of the mountaineers and evaluates the vast body of fiction written about them, earned a citation for distinguished scholarship from the board of Regents of New York University when Williams was awarded the Ph.D. degree in 1961. A revised edition of the dissertation appeared serially in *Appalachian Journal* and was republished as a book by the Appalachian Consortium Press of Boone, North Carolina.

From 1938 to 1941 Williams was the principal and a teacher of English at Louisa High School, which had been consolidated with the Lawrence County School System in 1936. At Louisa he developed a testing program and one of the first school-wide guidance and counseling programs in Kentucky.

After a year in industry, he left the Apprentice School of International Nickel Corporation in Huntington, West Virginia, to join the faculty of Appalachian State Teachers College at Boone, North Carolina, in 1942. At Appalachian he was for four years a critic teacher in English in the Demonstration High School, director of dramatics, assistant principal, and the director of the guidance and counseling program, which he developed and which was one of the first school-wide programs in North Carolina.

From 1946 to 1958 he was a teacher of English, speech, and dramatics at Appalachian. During those years he directed the productions of Playcrafters, was the faculty adviser for the student newspaper, the first faculty director of the artists and lecture series, and a member of several faculty committees.

Williams became dean of the graduate school at Appalachian in 1958 and served in that position for 16 1/2 years, during which time the graduate school grew from a resident enrollment of 42 to 930 students and from five to thirty-one master's degree programs. The Board of Trustees named the graduate school for Dr. Williams after his retirement.

In addition to his responsibilities at what became in 1967 Appalachian State University, Dr. Williams served on the Planning and Policies Committee of the Council of Graduate Schools in the United States, was for ten years one of three consultants to the Committee on Graduate Studies of the American Association of State Colleges and Universities, and was a member of the Executive Committee of the Council of Southern Graduate Schools. He was a member of the committee that developed the nationally accepted guidelines for the Education Specialist (6th-year) degree and for the Doctor of Arts degree. He was also a member of the Academic Policies Committee for the North Carolina Board of Higher Education, replaced in 1971 by the Board of Governors of the University of North Carolina, which includes the sixteen state institutions. He was also a member of the Teacher Certification Committee of the North Carolina Board of Public Instruction.

Dr. Williams was acting vice chancellor for academic affairs at Appalachian State University in 1974 and acting chancellor in 1975. He retired on July 1, 1976, after 46 years as teacher and administrator, but is continuing at Appalachian on a part-time basis as special assistant to the chancellor. On the eve of his retirement

Appalachian State University held in his honor a three-day Appalachian symposium, at which scholars from across the nation read papers and gave lectures on subjects relating to Appalachia. Selected papers were published in *An Appalachian Symposium: Essays Written in Honor of Cratis D. Williams*, edited by J.W. Williamson and published by the university of 1977. The Appalachian Studies Conference grew out of the symposium.

In 1937 Cratis Williams married Sylvia Graham, an English teacher, poet, and amateur actress. A native of Cherokee in Lawrence County, Kentucky, Sylvia was a graduate of the academy at Berea College and of Morehead State Teachers College (University). She died in 1942. In 1949 he married Elizabeth Lingerfelt of Athens, Tennessee, a graduate of East Tennessee State University. They are the parents of David C. Williams, a teacher at Wake Forest University, and Sophie Williams, a student at the School of Nursing of Boise State University in Idaho.

Dr. Williams' articles on mountain speech and idiom appeared over a ten-year period in *Mountain Life and Work*, published by the Council of the Southern Mountains with headquarters at the time on the campus of Berea College. In addition he has been a member of the editorial boards of *Mountain Life and Work*, *The Appalachian South*, *North Carolina Folklore*, *Appalachian Faculty Publications*, and is advising editor of the *Appalachian Journal*. He has contributed to these publications as well as to *Kentucky Folklore Record*, *Journal of American Folklore*, *Shenandoah*, *Appalachian Heritage*, *North Carolina Literary and Historical Review*, and a number of educational journals.

He is, or has been, a member of MLA, SAMLA, the North Carolina English Teachers Association, the North Carolina Literary and Historical Association, The National Education Association, the American Folklore Society, the North Carolina Folklore Society (past president), the Kentucky Folklore Society, the Southern Historical Association, the Western North Carolina Historical

Association, and the Historical Society of North Carolina, before which he has read papers on the cultural history of North Carolina mountaineers. Recently, he completed a five-year term as a member of the North Carolina Humanities Committee and is presently a member of the North Carolina Folk Life Committee, the board of directors of the Appalachian Consortium, the executive committee of the Western North Carolina Historical Association, the executive committee of the Watauga County Historical Society, the board of

A lecture on southern mountain speech.   MSU   Photo.

directors of the Hindman Settlement school, and the board of Consultants of Appalshop at Whitesburg, Kentucky.

In 1972 Dr. Williams was the recipient of the annual award of the Western North Carolina Historical Association in recognition of his contributions to scholarship on the history and folk traditions of Appalachia. He received in 1973 the prestigious O. Max Gardner Award for distinguished contributions to the welfare of the human race, given annually by the Board of Governors of the University of

North Carolina. In 1975 he received the Outstanding Alumnus Award of Cumberland College and was a recipient of the Brown-Hudson Award of the North Carolina Folklore Society, which recognized him as "Master Folklorist of Appalachia." He was the *Raleigh News and Observer's* Tar Heel of the Week in June 1976, and received the Appalachian Consortium's Laurel Leaves Award for Distinguished Service in July 1976. He was awarded the Doctor of Humane Letters degree by Berea College in 1977. In May 1980 he received Berea College's Special W. D. Weatherford Award for published work that in a significant way furthers understanding of Appalachian people.

Although he is untrained in music, Dr. Williams has received wide acclaim for the faithfulness of his presentation of the singing tradition of mountaineers. Popular as an entertainer and commentator on the mountaineers, he has appeared on programs for clubs, societies, colleges, universities, conventions, workshops, church groups, and cultural associations from New York to Florida. In 1982 he gave a lecture on Appalachia at the World's Fair in Knoxville and delivered the commencement address at Cumberland College.

Dr. Williams is listed in *Who's Who in America, Who's Who in Education, Directory of American Scholars*, and *Lawles's 100 American Folk Song Singers*.

[1]Cratis D. Williams to James M. Gifford, September 15, 1983.

MSU Photo.

MSU Photo.

A Humanist Reviews His Life

Several weeks ago you asked me for a statement about myself[2] and my odyssey from the happy innocence of a secure childhood in the cultural and social context of an Appalachian valley through troubling adventures of doubt, challenges to selfhood, denial, shame, and rejection, to understanding, acceptance, and affirmation of self as an Appalachian person who embraces his culture, searches out its history, and is proud of his identity as an Appalachian without feeling that he is therefore something less as an American for being an Appalachian.

That I found again something of the security I enjoyed as an Appalachian before I left the community in which I grew up while advancing through the humanities to a Ph.D. in an eastern university and in my profession from one-room school teacher in the mountains of Kentucky to university president without compromising my integrity as a humanist and obscuring my identity as an Appalachian means, it seems to me, that there is sustenance in the culture of the hills "from whence cometh my strength."

As a humanistic interpreter of my culture and as a teacher, speaker, entertainer, and writer, I feel that I have helped hundreds of other Appalachians toward self-acceptance and pride in who they are. I am most gratified that my sustained effort over many years helped to mount burgeoning Appalachian studies in school and college curricula throughout the region and inspired sincere scholarly reevaluation of America's most easily identified and possibly most significant subculture. It pleases me that nearly 400 doctoral dissertations have been written about Appalachia since 1965, for it is beginning to seem to me that 15 million Appalachians might soon lift their heads proudly in self-acceptance as they embrace their heritage.

In my childhood in a remote mountain valley relatively untouched by outside influences I played in my grandfather's distillery; heard my mother and my grandmother sing ballads and tell tales in the old prototypical dialect of the mountains, essentially the same that had been brought from Lowland Scotland to Ulster in the early 1600s and on into Appalachia immediately following the American Revolution; went to a hard-shell church where hymns were sung in Gregorian fashion and sermons were chanted; played traditional singing games at school and Sunday gatherings; danced for my grandfather when he played his banjo; went to annual funeralizings at family graveyards; attended family reunions; helped my father gather herbs for family medicine; gathered chestnuts and hickory nuts with cousins; hunted and trapped; listened to patriarchs tell of family kinship ties; followed Civil War soldiers about on Sunday afternoons to hear them swap tales about the war; and worked in the fields, beginning at age six, with my father.

It was a comfortable but at the same time an exciting world in which I lived as a child. I saw women riding on side saddles and carrying baskets of eggs to country stores, mules loaded with great bags of wool being taken to a carding mill, horseback riders, buggies and surreys on the dusty trails. I saw grooms and their brides riding to their "in fares" [the "in-fare" was a wedding dinner and party in the home of the groom]. Peddlers of all kinds came, including basket makers and housewives selling salves and patent medicines. Travelers who stopped to spend the night with us talked far into the night.

April 5, 1925—14th birthday.

Courtesy of the Williams Family Collection.

We went to workings, bean-stringings, corn-shellings, where sometimes we could square dance ("run the sets" or have "play parties"), and during the hog-killing time we swapped work with neighbors. The schoolmasters, none of whom had gone to high school, spoke the Appalachian speech along with the rest of us, but many of them were excellent teachers.

There was also violence in the community. I witnessed many family fights and saw bloody encounters on the "church grounds." I saw bleeding men dying after gun battles. My teacher during the third grade was shot and killed at church one Sunday. But for all the violence and display of mean temper it never occurred to me that I was living in a "dangerous" place, even though an average of two a year in the community during the decade of the 1920s were involved in killings.

At the age of twelve I rode on my father's farm wagon out of my valley to school in Louisa, the county-seat town, 25 miles from my home and psychologically as far away as San Francisco is from Frankfort today. What I found at school was a jolt to me. I was shamed by my English teacher and laughed at by my fellow students. Obviously, I was to reject my culture and deny my identity, which I was able to do within a few months, but I felt unreal. The real me stood within the shadows to monitor as I asked myself from time to time, "How am I doing?" For the long Christmas holiday seasons and the summers I returned to my valley, where people were real but where it was important that I prove to everybody that going away to school had not changed me in any way. Returning for a few months each year into the culture in which I had grown up led in time to my reevaluating it.

By the time I was a senior in high school I was beginning to speak positively for the Appalachian culture, to collect ballads and songs, and to read what I could find about Appalachia.

In college I picked up from professors and students from

outside the Appalachian region the negative attitudes toward us Appalachians that fictional stereotypes had created. It was a shame to be Appalachian. An Appalachian person's first obligation to himself was to identify and correct or reject everything about himself that betrayed his identity. As I considered and tried alternates, I found many of them superficial, unreal, often pretentious, and sometimes hypocritical. I had to pretend, for example, that young middle-class women were innocent little girls who played at life as if they were still in doll houses. I had to substitute shallow euphemisms for the colorful and vigorous language in my dialect. People played religion in middle-class churches and few seemed to take it very seriously. In time I was pleased to discover that my advancement in liberal studies had taken me also beyond middle-class concerns, which I felt no need to reject or attack or criticize, for they had never been vital to me anyway.

MSU Photo.

As a teacher, principal, university professor, administrator, I found that I could honestly tolerate without feeling compelled to attack social agencies and institutions and that I could work with students, fellow teachers, and administrators with backgrounds much different from my own without "putting anybody down." My good will and spirit of tolerance were the foundation stones of my "educational statesmanship." My acceptance of people as they themselves saw themselves stood me in good stead.

My ability to listen, consider, ask questions without condemning or rejecting appealed to those whose fate it was to work with me. It has seemed to me that such success as I might have enjoyed as a "public person" is owing largely to my having accepted myself with confidence, and without significant loss of self-esteem, as an Appalachian. I never feel the need to apologize for who I am or to try to obscure my identity. I find it enormously comfortable to be myself.

[2] This autobiographical statement was part of a grant proposal to fund a film project entitled "Cratis Williams: A Complete Mountaineer." Cratis Williams to Jo Crockett Zingg, November 2, 1981.

1944—While at Appalachian High School.
Courtesy of the Williams Family Collection.

Proper Name Index